More Praise for *Secrets of Great Marriages*

"This book is an invaluable resource for supporting increased longevity and growth of mature and deep love in the sacred crucible of marriage. Once again, the authors provide an honest assessment of what is troublesome, challenging, and difficult as well as what is good, true, and beautiful within a marriage. Nowhere else will you find a book that addresses marriage in such a thorough and comprehensive way. It is practical, useful, inspirational, humorous, and invaluable in its contribution to all who value and explore committed relationship."

— Angeles Arrien, PhD, cultural anthropologist and author of
The Second Half of Life

"The Blooms' commitment to relationship — demonstrated by their many years together and their fine undertaking in *Secrets of Great Marriages* — is certainly commendable. The couples in this book eloquently describe the relationship roller coaster, offering very enjoyable lessons that give readers an opportunity to compare notes with others on the same path."

— Stephen and Ondrea Levine, authors of *Embracing the Beloved*

"Almost as universal as our desire for love is the skepticism about whether a long-term loving relationship is possible. By going to the 'experts' — couples who know how to make it happen because they have made it happen — this book gives us both inspiration and practical ideas for attaining real and lasting love."

— Jordan Paul, PhD, coauthor of *Do I Have to Give Up Me
to Be Loved By You?* and author of *Becoming Your Own Hero*

"This is a wonderfully read~~ble~~ ~~~~ at are both heart-warming and instruc~~~~ t it's like for other people. What are th~~~~ est of? And how do they deal with the ~~~~ like sex, money, and parenting? I have ~~~~ ~~~~g some of the ideas presented here to enhance ~~~~ ~~~~onship."

— Susan Campbell, PhD, author of *Getting Real* and *The Couple's Journey*

"While the secrets of successful marriages are being demystified by contemporary scientific scrutiny, most of the data comes from studying conflicted, often dysfunctional, marriages. The portraits of couples in *Secrets of Great*

Marriages demystify the intimate bond by studying successful rather than conflicted couples and identifying the factors they all have in common. Any couple reading these stories will be inspired, challenged, and guided toward the relationship of their dreams. I highly recommend it to all couples, successful or unsuccessful."

— Harville Hendrix, PhD, author of *Getting the Love You Want*

"With this entrancing book, once again the Blooms work their special magic of evoking, appreciating, and analyzing the special alchemy of relationships and their power to test, heal, and transform us throughout life. Each couple in this living collection is vividly unique — and each is marked by common depths of respect, mutual appreciation, and commitment to a life of learning and growth, which carries them through crises and challenges to fulfillment and new horizons. Read, laugh, and weep in recognition — and learn nuggets you can use immediately in your own practice and your own life."

— Gordon Wheeler, PhD, president of Esalen Institute
and author of *Beyond Individualism*

Praise for *101 Things I Wish I Knew When I Got Married*

"Practical, easy-to-understand nuggets that can help every marriage grow."
— Gerald G. Jampolsky, MD, author of *Love Is Letting Go of Fear*

"Filled with many wise words on sustaining love in marriage.... The Blooms are fine guides to making love last."

— *Spirituality & Health*

"Marriage counselors and first-time authors, the Blooms nearly called their union quits in 1987; their anecdotes reflect the 'acceptance, gratitude, and appreciation' that they employed to save it. Some of these honest, candid stories (many from the authors) are more illustrative than others, but most vividly demonstrate that successful relationships require effort."

— *Library Journal*

"We're enchanted by the pearls of marital wisdom in *101 Things I Wish I Knew When I Got Married*."

— *Bridal Guide*

"Well written and a pleasure to read."

— *Church & Synagogue Libraries*

SECRETS
OF GREAT
MARRIAGES

SECRETS OF GREAT MARRIAGES

Real Truth from Real Couples about Lasting Love

Charlie and Linda Bloom

Foreword by John Robbins

New World Library
Novato, California

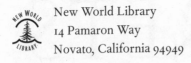

New World Library
14 Pamaron Way
Novato, California 94949

Text design by Tona Pearce Myers

Library of Congress Cataloging-in-Publication Data
Bloom, Charlie.
  Secrets of great marriages : real truth from real couples about lasting love / Charlie and Linda Bloom ; foreword by John Robbins.
     p.   cm.
  ISBN 978-1-57731-678-7 (pbk. : alk. paper)
  1. Marriage. I. Bloom, Linda. II. Title.
  HQ734.B6572 2010
  306.81—dc22   2009043050

First printing, February 2010
ISBN 978-1-57731-678-7
Printed in Canada on 100% postconsumer-waste recycled paper

g New World Library is a proud member of the Green Press Initiative.

10 9 8 7 6 5 4 3 2 1

CONTENTS

FOREWORD

I'm proud of Charlie and Linda Bloom for writing this book because it's a different kind of book. It doesn't promise that you will have an extraordinary relationship if only you follow a particular set of rules. Instead, it offers the hard-earned and authentic wisdom of couples who speak in their own voices of their struggles and growth. The result is life-giving because it affirms the possibility of creating joyous and honest relationships that serve the deepest life purposes of each partner. In story after story, you see the miracles that occur when two hearts unite.

The people who share their words and insights here are passionately alive. They don't all have interests in common with their partners, but they are interesting people in their own right, so they bring vitality into the marriage. They have achieved a delicate balance: they are committed to themselves and to the relationship; and they care about their own needs and those of their partners in equal measure, neither putting their own needs first nor sacrificing their needs to attend to their partners'.

These are real couples telling the real truth. They have been successful not because they have had blissful, stress-free lives but because they have created relationships that gave them strength during their most anguishing trials and enabled them to emerge from their hardships more whole, freer, and more fully themselves. They have been faced with every conceivable challenge and difficulty, but they were willing to pay their dues, to keep nourishing the relationship, to adjust and adapt as circumstances changed. All the partners have given a lot of themselves to their marriage, unwilling to settle for an "okay" relationship.

While the Blooms were writing this book and conducting these interviews, they went on a cruise and met a couple celebrating their fiftieth anniversary. Despite the happy occasion, the couple seemed morose, bitter, and critical of each other. Charlie and Linda asked them what they attributed the longevity of their relationship to. "Grin and bear it," the woman answered sourly. This attitude is the antithesis of what is embodied by the couples in this book. None of them are staying in a marriage merely for comfort and security. They are seeking growth and consciousness. They are willing to take chances. They are brave in their intimacy with each other.

One of the things that makes the Blooms' work so empowering is that they see that there is no single correct way to be in a marriage. Rather, there is a nearly infinite variety of paths, depending on the two people who are creating the contract. The Blooms recognize that each couple is unique and has its own journey of love, healing, and transformation. Reading their book has opened my eyes to the many different arrangements and agreements that couples have developed to enhance and support what they are committed to creating together. They remind us that a marriage is whatever the people who are involved agree that it is.

The Blooms let the stories of these great relationships stand on their own merit. You don't have to emulate any of them, and you certainly don't have to replicate a formula that has been historically identified as the proper form for marriage. Instead, you have the opportunity to develop your own creative form of partnership. This is liberating, indeed. You can create whatever best meets your unique needs and interests, and those of your partner. Marriage can be a forum for possibilities that enrich not only the couple but also everyone they encounter.

These days, to form a highly functioning, deeply intimate, and creative partnership and a truly happy family is an act of heroism. It means not allowing yourself or your relationship to be shaped by the prevailing drift of the culture. It means recognizing how much care and attention relationships require. It means facing your problems together. It doesn't mean sugarcoating harsh realities. It means leaning into the challenges you face without accusations or blame. As one of the couples puts it, the way to avoid divorce is to have a no-fault marriage.

Of course, not all relationships are meant to last forever. Some of the people in this book were married before, and those marriages ended in divorce. One man and his wife tried for years to fix a marriage that wasn't working, and they spent thousands of dollars in marriage therapy. But for reasons that neither of them could control, they weren't able to develop the kind of connection that would sustain them, and eventually they realized that it would be an act of disrespect to stay in an unharmonious marriage. However, they managed to learn what they needed from the experience so they didn't blindly repeat the same patterns in their subsequent relationships.

If you are in a challenging relationship and you don't know whether it's worth hanging in there, here's what the Blooms suggest: Give it your absolute best shot. Get the finest professional help you can get. Practice the best relationship skills you can. Try to undo the old patterns that are holding you back. Speak the truth without judgment, and risk trying new things. Do everything you can to be something greater than a reaction machine. Work to hone the skills that make you eligible for a great relationship.

You can only benefit from doing this hard, deliberate, and intentional work, because one of two outcomes will happen: either things will turn around, or it will become abundantly clear that they aren't going to improve. Either way, you will then be clear about what needs to happen next. If you do your best and it's still not working, you can leave with your head high and your back straight. You will have nurtured the relationship as much as possible, and you won't be haunted with regret.

One couple in this book found their relationship to be in a dire condition. They each felt trapped in feelings of disconnection, emptiness, resentment, and despair. They tried to work it out but realized that they had to let go of their identity as a couple in order to become whole, self-reliant, and free of crippling codependence. They divorced and went their completely separate ways. But four years later they reconnected, and because both had been doing the work they needed to do, they found that they could now meet in an entirely new way. They remarried and created the kind of relationship they had each always wanted but been unable to create in the first instance.

Reading this book has been a great pleasure because it repeatedly captured my imagination. As I read, I identified first with this couple, and then with that one, feeling that if they managed to deal in such positive and successful ways with the challenges and hardships they encountered, then maybe I could too.

My wife and I have been married for forty-three years, and we greatly enjoy reading the book out loud to each other. Each time we do, we find new insights and ideas that enliven our connection and help us to feel closer to ourselves both as individuals and as part of our intimate partnership. Each time, we gain a sense of hopefulness and some very practical ideas about how to work creatively with the difficulties inherent in marriage.

Whether you are in a shaky relationship or a fabulous one, or not in one at all, this book can show you the skills and commitments necessary for creating a partnership that sustains over the long haul.

— John Robbins, author of
The New Good Life and *Diet for a New America*

ACKNOWLEDGMENTS

Our deepest appreciation goes first and foremost to the couples who participated in this project. Getting to know them as intimately as we have has been a peak experience in our lives. We will be forever grateful to those whose stories are in the completed version of the book, as well as to those whose stories are not. All the stories were moving and inspiring, but because of the space available, essential points that needed to be made were better illustrated by some stories than by others. We're profoundly appreciative to all the couples for their willingness to share so generously and extensively their time and wisdom. We also thank our clients, and those couples in our workshops throughout our years of doing seminar facilitation, who assisted us in understanding and appreciating what goes into the creation of great marriages. We have done our best to present these stories with sensitivity and accuracy in order to preserve not only the factual information of these couples' lives together but also the feeling level and tone of their experiences as they were revealed to us.

We are also indebted to our friends who expressed their support and generosity to us through their frank and honest feedback and editorial suggestions. Special thanks in particular to David Kerns, MD, and John and Deo Robbins for taking time away from their own writing projects to enhance ours with their insights and wisdom. We also thank Gordon Wheeler and Nancy Lunney Wheeler and the Esalen Institute, and Denise Barack and the Kripalu Center, for believing in our work with unconditional support and for sponsoring our work-shops and seminars over the years.

And we thank our children, Jesse and Sarah, and our daughter-in-law, Cassia, for their appreciation and support of our work, particularly during those times when it removed us from the family. The extraordinarily wonderful adults you have become reassure us that any difficulties that may have arisen during those times have left no scars. We stand in awe and deepest appreciation of the beautiful beings that you continue to evolve into. And special thanks to Devin, our first grandchild, who has for the past two years lit up our lives in ways that no words can adequately express.

Thanks also to the many teachers and guides along the path who lent us their wisdom, eloquence, humor, and inspiration, particularly Stephen and Ondrea Levine, Ram Dass, Sylvia and Seymour Boorstein, and Jack Kornfield. You have all served as beacons of light to us, especially during times that were dark and confusing. A huge "thank you" to our copyeditor, Bonita Hurd. Much gratitude goes to Georgia Hughes, our most excellent editor, who believed in this book even during those times when our own conviction wavered, and whose editorial expertise is of the highest order. And finally, thanks to Marc Allen, founder and publisher of New World Library, for your willingness to embody your commitment to global transformation through your work, your vision, and your integrity.

INTRODUCTION

The idea for this book began about ten years ago after we heard countless clients, students, friends, and colleagues lament that "there are just no good, available men/women out there, and hardly anyone has a decent relationship anyway," or words to that effect. We decided that someday we would write a book that would disprove the many naysayers who seemed determined to confirm their belief that good relationships are simply impossible for any save the fortunate few who, for unknown reasons, were lucky enough to have found their soul mates.

We vowed that we would even reveal the secrets of "fortunate" souls that enabled them to create not only good marriages but great ones. We would interview people who met our criteria for fulfilling relationships and share their stories in a way that would both inspire readers and illuminate the key factors that made these couples' success possible. And we would do it all without delivering the long lists of dos and don'ts and other commandments that self-help books are famous for. The book that you are holding represents the results of that commitment.

The statistics for successful marriages haven't changed much since we started working with couples in the mid-1970s. Slightly over 50 percent of first marriages still end in divorce, and about 60 percent of second marriages do. Despite the thousands of books, tapes, CDs, DVDs, and workshops about creating successful relationships, and the countless millions of dollars spent on therapy and marriage counseling, the numbers haven't changed much. We are neither presumptuous nor arrogant enough to claim that this book will completely reverse this trend. We do believe, however, that it contains wisdom that, if taken to heart, has the potential to inspire and transform the lives of couples who otherwise might add to the list of casualties represented by divorce statistics. Although the stories in this book may not change the world, they can change at least one life: yours.

There are reasons why such a low percentage of married couples fail to achieve the quality of life together they hoped for when they decided to marry. It's not necessarily for lack of trying, lack of motivation, lack of intentionality, or lack of desire that marriages so frequently fail. So why do they fail? The abbreviated answer is simply that sharing two lives intimately and cooperatively requires skills, knowledge, and inner strengths that most of us have not developed by the time we become a part of a couple. Relationship skills take time, effort, discipline, and work to cultivate and refine, usually more than we realize and often more than we are prepared to provide. But if you wait until you have mastered the relationship game before you create a committed partnership, you'll probably die of old age first. The time to learn the lessons is not before you get into a relationship, it's while you're in one. In the words of one person we spoke to, "It's *all* on-the-job training!"

The couples in this book are no exception to this rule. They all came into marriage with a lot to learn, whether they were marriage counselors themselves or blue-collar workers. This book is not about what makes these couples special, because, as they would all acknowledge, they are not, but about what has enabled them to create the lives together that they have. It's about how ordinary people can create extraordinary relationships, regardless of their level of education, quality of childhood experience, family background, and relationship history. And it's about how these couples have managed to fulfill the paradoxical mandate of great marriages: that each must give fully and generously to the other without losing his or her own integrity, or sense of wholeness, in the process.

While this may seem daunting, it is nonetheless do-able for those willing to embrace the vast range of opportunities that marriage offers. These couples' heartfelt stories illuminate some of the infinite variety of ways in which the challenges of marriage can be met.

Our first challenge was to come up with criteria for selecting the couples. Many people claim to be happily married, but this phrase has been overused and generalized to the point that it is now practically meaningless. Couples who identify themselves as happily married could be merely tolerating each other, or passionately in love with each other, or something in between. We knew what we were looking for, and we were confident that we would know it when we saw it, but we weren't sure how to precisely characterize the nature of the relationship we were looking for. In the end we decided to begin with seven couples we knew well enough to be sure they had the kind of relationship we wanted to include in the book. We looked at what it was about them that made us feel that way, and we came up with several factors they had in common. We found that both partners:

- Have a high level of mutual respect and trust.
- Have good conflict management skills and work out differences effectively.
- Have a nonhierarchical relationship: they treat each other as equals.
- Tend not to hold grudges.
- Have a low tolerance for unfinished business, and when differences arise, they address issues quickly rather than put them on the back burner.
- Tend not to get caught in cycles of blame, and generally look at their own contributions to relationship breakdowns when they occur.
- Are comfortable expressing and acknowledging their affection and need for each other and do so freely.
- Frequently acknowledge what they appreciate about each other and express their complaints or concerns respectfully without making the other seem wrong.

- Are honest with themselves and each other.
- Take pleasure in bringing happiness into each other's life and frequently engage in acts of service to each other.
- Find meaning and purpose in their individual lives through activities, interests, and commitments they are passionate about.
- Take great pleasure in each other's company, yet do not derive their sense of wholeness as individuals from their relationship.
- Characterize themselves as having a loving and deeply fulfilling marriage.
- Have been together as a couple for at least fifteen years. (The average length of time these couples have been together is thirty-one years.)

Recommendations for other couples we might interview came from the friends and colleagues we told about our project, as well as from some of the original seven couples we started with. Within two months we had a long list of potential candidates. In the end, we got more than a hundred recommendations, and with these couples we made at least initial contact. We ended up interviewing fifty-two couples, twenty-seven of whom are included here. The next stage of the process involved the actual interviews. We've chosen to allow the interviews to speak for themselves, rather than try to distill the essence of the couples' words into a series of guidelines or specific "shoulds" for creating great relationships. We trusted, and continue to trust, the transformative power of stories, and are confident that, when people speak the truth of their experiences, whatever needs to be revealed will be brought forth.

Although this project arose out of our intention to serve others by providing stories we hoped would be both instructive and illuminating, we didn't anticipate the degree to which we would be inspired and moved by the eloquence and honesty of these couples. Their willingness to reveal some of their most intimate experiences, and their feelings related to those experiences, moved us at times to tears. It became clear early on that these people were not simply *talking about* the qualities that characterize outstanding relationships, such as commitment, vulnerability, humility, integrity, honesty, and generosity, but actually embodying those qualities and bringing them to our shared experience as we spoke together. We have learned more from them than we had imagined possible. As a result, we are wiser, more openhearted, and more hopeful than we were before writing this book. It is our sincere hope that as a result of reading it, you will be too.

1.

IT'S NEVER TOO LATE
TO HEAL OLD WOUNDS

Pete and Deanna Smith

Pete Smith is as down-to-earth as his name suggests. As regular a guy as you'll ever meet, Pete is a genuine Down-Easterner who has lived and worked on the sea nearly all his life. A lobsterman by trade, he knows the waters off the shore of Maine like his own backyard. He is as comfortable in his small lobster boat, even when storms whip up the Atlantic, as most people are on dry land. It takes a lot to rattle him. But back in 1968, when he served as a soldier in Vietnam, Pete got rattled, big time. And although he managed to survive an ordeal that many soldiers didn't, the ghosts of Vietnam never stopped haunting him. Some things are just too big to permanently put away. At least that's what Pete told himself when his nightmares and flashbacks periodically returned to upset his sleep and shatter his peace of mind.

Never did Pete imagine it would be a woman who would help redeem him from the demons that were granting him no rest. He also never imagined that he would return to the place that he had spent years trying to erase from his memory. Pete and Deanna's story is a testament to the transformative power of love. It is a lesson in the healing potential of true compassion and a reminder that miracles occur when there is a union of two hearts.

In being an integral part of Pete's healing, Deanna discovered an aspect of herself that she hadn't previously known existed. She came to see that her life purpose was much greater than simply supporting herself and fulfilling the obligations that go along with being a responsible adult. In committing herself to supporting her husband, Deanna experienced a spiritual awakening that altered not only her personal identity but also the way she related to the world. She discovered, as so many others have, that in supporting the healing of another, we ourselves are also healed. And to heal is to become more whole.

It wasn't what Deanna said to Pete or what she did for him when his demons raged the loudest. It was the steady, openhearted presence that she invited him into that reassured him he was no longer alone in facing them. The steadfast presence of someone who loves us makes what we cannot tolerate bearable. Toward the end of our conversation, Deanna said, "Pete wasn't the only one healed by our relationship; I was too." Pete reached over to take Deanna's hand. His smile said it all.

PETE: I make my living as a lobsterman living in a small fishing village in Maine. I'm self-employed, and I've been running my own boat for more than twenty years. It's a small operation with three hundred traps, which requires a crew of at least two to man the boat. Several years ago, I lost my stern-man and was searching for a replacement. I put the word out that I needed a crewman, and within a few days, I got a response from this woman named Deanna.

When she applied for the job, I thought she was kidding. I'd never had a woman on my crew, never even heard of such a thing. Nowadays there are a lot of women working all kinds of jobs in the business, some even running their own boats, but back then it was pretty much unheard of.

DEANNA: I had been working as a children's librarian and wanted a change. I wasn't daunted by Pete's insistence that lobstering was hard work and that I may not be up to it. I didn't see any reason why I couldn't work on a lobster boat, but I had some reservations of my own. I didn't want to work for some irresponsible cowboy — God knows there were plenty of them out there. I checked into his references too.

PETE: She was young, attractive, and slim, but I could tell she had strong arms. That's important on a lobster boat. She also had a strong character. It was clear from the way she answered my questions that Deanna wasn't afraid of a challenge. After we spoke, I made the decision to take her on. A stern-person works the back of the boat behind the skipper. It's a tough job, but Deanna could haul traps with the best of 'em. She picked it up really quick. Deanna proved to be an excellent crewmember. She mastered the job quickly and was one of the most competent and reliable employees I had ever had. She was also, hands down, the most beautiful, inside and out.

DEANNA: The very first day I worked on the boat, we spent nine hours together. Pete was so easy to talk to. He's a great listener, and he has a terrific sense of humor. I thought to myself, "What a nice guy." He was open, honest, sociable, and full of compassion. Our relationship soon went from being that of coworkers to that of friends, then best friends, and eventually lovers. Within six months we were living together, and a few months later we got married. I've never had a moment's doubt or a dull moment.

PETE: Although I didn't understand why, the subject that I kept coming back to in our conversations was my experience as a helicopter crew chief in Vietnam in the late sixties. Although the war had ended decades earlier, I still would wake up in the middle of the night trembling from my flashbacks and nightmares. Deanna held and comforted me with such tenderness. No one had ever done that for me before. Sometimes she sang gentle songs in that sweet voice of hers and would lull me back to sleep.

I had never talked to anyone about my experience in Vietnam. After my tour of duty, I'd had trouble holding down jobs and had a hard time with friendships. There was so much lingering anger and fear that I was exhausted a lot of the time. Finally I decided to see a psychologist at the Veteran's Administration Hospital. I'd had a good childhood, and my ex-wife and I were getting along well with each other. I knew that the trouble I was having was about Vietnam. All the VA offered me was medication, but I knew that wasn't what I needed. Twenty-five minutes into the interview with the psychologist, I told him, "Look, I don't know any guys who have done such a thing, but I know that when I get bucked off a horse I need to get back on it. Give me a plane ticket back to Vietnam, and I'll find some healing for myself." He didn't buy it, and neither did anyone else at the hospital. They just wanted to drug me. I knew what I needed, and it wasn't drugs.

DEANNA: When Pete told me what had happened at the hospital, I asked him if he really wanted to go to Vietnam, and he simply said, "Yes." So at the end of the lobstering season, we took the boat out of the water, and I purchased plane tickets for us. Everyone thought we were nuts.

PETE: I came home one day to find two packed suitcases, and all of a sudden it all started to get very real. Right about then my stomach started doing flip-flops.

DEANNA: We headed out without much of an idea about what we would do or even exactly where we would go. We just knew we had to go. When we got to Hanoi, Pete started to get really scared. I told him that anytime he felt he had to leave Vietnam, we would just get on a plane and go.

PETE: When we landed, I began to get the shakes. Old memories that I had been blocking out for years started pouring back. Although we had been prepared ahead of time for the fact that when we arrived our passports would be taken, when they actually reached over to take mine, I freaked out. "You're not going to take my passport!" I screamed. A very kindly, local guide came over to me, took me aside, and gently put his arm around my shoulders saying, "Pete, when in Rome, do as the Romans do. It's all right." His manner reassured me to the point where I could give them my passport.

DEANNA: The central highland was the place where Pete had flown every day for six months. During that time, dozens of people he knew were injured or killed. After we had been in Vietnam for about two weeks, we hired a driver to take us up north to the major battle sites, where the worst carnage took place. All day — during the day and into the night — as he anticipated going there, Pete was sweating profusely. He couldn't stop shaking. His stomach hurt so much he could barely stand up.

PETE: It was as if the old fear and tension I had felt during the fighting had been stashed in my tissues, and it was now back in full force. I told Deanna that I wasn't sure I could go through with the trip to the battle sites. She reassured me that we would do only what I was up to doing. I felt so naked and vulnerable. I was afraid to go, but something inside me kept saying that I had to see this thing through. We hired a guide who had taken other veterans back to the places of their nightmares. The night before we went up there, things got really bad. I was sweating and shaking out of control. I got down on my knees and prayed to my higher power to help me get through this ordeal. I said, "I'm ready for whatever you have in store for me."

To restore your soul, you may have to risk losing your mind

PETE: Driving through the jungle, up and down ravines, I was overwhelmed with emotion and found myself reliving some old events. It was as if the old memories and my present-moment experience were blurring together. The driver told me that his father had been part of the Viet Cong. Everywhere I looked there were only Asian people. My mind associated Asian people with danger. I knew that the young driver hadn't even been alive when I was in the war, but I was catapulted back to a time when I was fighting for my life. I was terrified and thought he wanted to kill me. I kept flip-flopping back and forth between having a few moments of sanity and then insanity.

My paranoia was so great that I feared the people around us were all enemy agents. It all seemed so real that I actually wondered whether Deanna herself was part of the conspiracy. Later that night, I got out of bed and got down on my knees. There was a gecko on the ceiling making its noise. I was so out of it that I imagined the gecko was answering my prayers, and that his voice was saying, "All right. All right. It's going to be all right."

DEANNA: I just held Pete's hand and lay down beside him in the bed. He was a human vibrator — it was as if an electric current were going through his body. I just wanted to support him, but I knew he had to work it out inside himself. I kept reassuring him that it was safe. I trusted that the guides were sincere and they only meant to help us. I kept reminding Pete that if things got too intense, all he had to do was give me the word and we would leave. At one point he said, "Why don't we just forget this?" I said: "Fine, let's forget the whole thing and go home." But as soon as I said that, Pete insisted that he had to go through with it.

PETE: We went to the place where my outfit lost a lot of men; a lot of my friends were killed there. To me, I was standing on sacred ground. I cried for the men in my platoon who didn't survive, and for the ones who were maimed, and for myself and all the others who have suffered such emotional distress for so many years. I cried and cried. Then finally the tears stopped. Something in me shifted, simply standing on that ground, I began to settle down. I felt like it was over, the mission was complete. It was successful. And it was one of the hardest things I'd ever done. I knew that it was over because everything looked different and felt different. I felt proud that I did complete the journey. I began to see our driver and guide in a whole new way. He was no longer a threat but a part of my healing. I felt great love for this man who had supported so many Vietnam veterans by taking them to the sites of their nightmares.

Even the worst transgressions can be redeemed by acts of kindness

DEANNA: I was moved beyond words by Pete's commitment and his courage. After we left the scene of the worst fighting, our driver offered to take us to an orphanage behind the old wooden church that Pete used to fly over every day. It now housed children ranging from infants up to those eighteen years of age. On the way over we stopped and bought 150 pens and 150 pencils to give the children who lived there. Once we arrived, we met with the head nun, Sister Juliana. She didn't speak English, but through an interpreter we asked how we could help. She was shy and afraid to ask us for too much.

PETE: All of sudden the trip was no longer about me. Now it was about the orphans. The orphanage had just experienced an outbreak of impetigo, and they needed ointment. They needed formula for the babies, and they were short of sleeping mats. Sister Juliana said that many of the children were small enough to sleep on half a mat, and that if we bought twenty, they could cut them in half and get more usage from them. Deanna took out five hundred dollars in cash and handed it to Sister Juliana. Deanna said, "Buy the children whatever you think they need."

Our time at the orphanage was the highlight of the trip for me. We have adopted that orphanage and sent money to them regularly. Helping the orphans is a way that I feel I can give back to a country that has been harmed so much by my own country. It is a way that I find some peace for the things I did when I was still just a kid. It is part of the way I heal. Going back to Vietnam was an essential step of my recovery. I can't find the words to express the gratitude I feel toward Deanna for creating the opportunity for me to come to terms with my greatest fears.

When we got back to the United States, I noticed a marked difference, and I could tell I was relieved of the pain I had carried all those years. Before the trip, when I would be driving down a mountain road shrouded in clouds, it would take me back to those feelings of dread I had when I flew the helicopter in Vietnam. I would have flashbacks that would affect my mood all day long. Even a loud bang like a door being slammed used to be enough to put me in a foul mood that could last all day. I became aware of the healing effects of going to Vietnam when I could drive down a mountain road shrouded in clouds and think, "Aren't those mountains beautiful."

Deanna has opened my life in a big way. She exposed me to things I had never known before. And she sings like an angel. We still work together on the boat, and she's also my best friend. I married my best friend!

2.

GREAT MARRIAGES REQUIRE
GREAT INTEGRITY

Sara Nelson and Danny Sheehan

Danny Sheehan was one of Washington's most eligible bachelors. As an accomplished civil liberties attorney, he had defended the *New York Times* in what became known as the Pentagon Papers case, as well as several well-known political activists, including Benjamin Spock, Dick Gregory, and the Berrigan brothers, during the Vietnam era. Danny had a long track record of winning tough cases. He also had a reputation as an attractive bachelor and, at thirty, was in no hurry to settle down. That is, until Sara Nelson walked in to his life. At the time, Sara was the national labor secretary for NOW (the National Organization for Women) and was called "Wonder Woman" by most of the people who knew her. "She just completely took over the room as soon as she walked in," Danny recalled. "She was brilliant, powerful, and incredibly dynamic. And she was, and is, absolutely gorgeous."

Sara left the meeting where they first met before she and Danny had a chance to say much to each other. But she was around long enough to make an impression that would forever alter his life. "That night I started calling all the women in my little black book, telling them that from now on our relationship would be platonic. I knew from the moment I laid eyes on her that Sara was the only woman I ever wanted to be with. And from that day forward, she was."

Not only has Danny remained true to his word for the past thirty-four years, but he also claims to have never even desired to be with another woman. "I'm clear that there isn't anyone else out there with whom I could experience what I do with Sara. She's given me more than I could even begin to describe. And the love that I have for her keeps getting stronger."

Love itself, no matter how deep, does not ensure a blissful, stress-free life. Sometimes it seems that those people who have been given the most love are tested the most, and in the case of Danny and Sara the tests were frequent and increasingly demanding. But their love, the foundation of their relationship, created a sanctuary that let them survive the challenges and grow in response to their ordeals. Their story reminds us that the healing power of love is greater than we can imagine, and that the heart provides more trustworthy guidance than the collected knowledge contained in a library of great books.

DANNY: When Sara and I met, I wasn't paying the slightest bit of attention to the idea of mating with anyone. Marriage was not in my plans. My parents had a bad marriage, and my father was an alcoholic. I had decided much earlier that political work would be the main focus of my life. I was the legal representative of a community of Jesuits involved with a broad range of political issues and was living with them on a large estate that was a former convent. The other men living there were all Jesuit priests. When I told them I had become a one-woman man, they seemed relieved. That was before Sara and I had even discussed our relationship. At that point we had only spoken twice.

SARA: At the time, I was experiencing a personal identity crisis. Although I was all fired up as a political activist, working hard for very little pay, a nagging voice in the back of my mind kept telling me that the most important parts of myself were not integrated into my life. I remember praying that I would find a progressive man who would meet me in both the political and spiritual aspects of my being. When I heard Danny speaking at a Karen Silkwood meeting at the National Council of Churches, I felt God was tapping me on the shoulder. I knew I had found my soul mate.

DANNY: Very early in our relationship, I told Sara that I didn't want her to ever feel trapped. I wanted her to be in it only if she really wanted to be. I didn't see any need for us to get any outside "authority" like the government or the church to sanction our relationship. The love we had was enough. One thing I've always appreciated most about our relationship is that we both have our own views, and we're both totally free. We don't stay together because of an external authority, but because we choose to, every day.

SARA: Preparing for the Silkwood trial, we were both working fourteen-hour days with seven national constituencies and a great team of investigators, litigators, and organizers. Suddenly, we found out that we were going to have a baby. For two workaholics, this was a paradigm shift of earthquake proportions. We had been so focused on political work that we hadn't ever thought about children.

DANNY: When I found out that Sara was pregnant, it all seemed right. It was absolutely clear to me that it was all going to work out.

Balancing family and work requires commitment, teamwork, imagination, and creativity

SARA: After our first son, Danny Paul, was born, I was determined to keep going in my political work. I remember nursing him while I was fund-raising for the Silkwood trial. He went everywhere with us. Danny and I were firmly grounded in the principles of family and collective life, and the people around us just got used to our having a baby with us wherever we went. Danny even took him into the judge's chambers a couple of times during the trial.

After the Silkwood victory, twelve of us founded the Christic Institute to continue doing national investigations, litigation, and grass-roots organizing. Two and a half years later, our son Daegan was born while we were in the final push of the campaign to pass the Equal Rights Amendment. We continued to remain deeply involved with social justice issues, and over time our team handled several major cases, including one against the Ku Klux Klan and one related to Three Mile Island. From the beginning, Danny and I worked as partners within the larger team. We often made presentations together and were able to use the differences in our personalities as assets and strengths in our work.

DANNY: In the eighties the institute became highly involved with the Iran-Contra case, which consumed an enormous amount of our time and energy. By then Sara was the executive director, working with fifty-five people on our staff, and I was running the investigations and litigation. We knew we needed some help in caring for our children while we were doing this work, and both of our brothers offered to come live and work with us. They are great guys, and the universe blessed us with the support we needed at the time.

It looked certain that we would win the Contra case, with all the evidence of wrongdoing we had presented, but a political alliance blocked the full revelation of facts to the public. When we tried to take the case to the Supreme Court, they refused to hear it.

SARA: When it became clear that the Supreme Court was not going to take on the Iran-Contra case, we knew we would have to close our institute. We were ordered to repay all the court costs, which totaled about $1.5 million. We had a staff of fifty-five people that we had to let go. We had to sell all our property, which by that time consisted of six buildings, including our own home. We were financially devastated and physically and emotionally exhausted. In addition to the loss of the case and the money, I suffered a loss that at the time felt even more painful to me: I lost my trust in the system. Up to that time, I had truly believed that, if officials are presented with the truth, if they can recognize injustice where it exists, ultimately the truth will prevail and wrongs will be righted. We had always operated from the belief that if you shine the light of the truth into the darkness, the darkness will disappear.

We had been betrayed by the institutions I had believed in my whole life. Everything we and our generation had stood for seemed to be going up in smoke. The worst part was that Danny was being attacked from all sides. I told him, "No matter what happens, I will never leave you, and we will not lose our faith."

Things may have to fall apart in order to come together

DANNY: We had to regroup. A friend of ours had a beautiful ranch in Santa Barbara that he didn't use much. He offered it to us, and it became a refuge for our family. I got a teaching job at UC Santa Barbara, and we brought the kids and our dog to California so we could rest and recover by the ocean. After the move, I realized I had fallen prey to the cultural myth that a man's value comes from what he does. I had been raised to be successful, to be a winner. I was hypercompetitive; losing was not in my vocabulary. I had been captain of the high school football team as a freshman, and I had graduated from Harvard College and Harvard Law School. Competition and success were in my blood.

I knew that what had happened was a huge injustice, but the world viewed it as a big defeat. The situation forced me to rethink and reassess my whole life, my work, and my values — even my identity. It was difficult, but it turned out to be an incredibly rich time of introspection for me, and a time of much richer connection with Sara and the boys. It was a time of healing and recovery for her too. I had to examine my beliefs and find out who I was, other than the litigator. We both became much more circumspect, and the spiritual dimension of our relationship began to grow much stronger. We realized that we had to go to higher ground to do the next phase of our work together.

Nature can be the best medicine

SARA: It had been such an emotionally stressful time, and we had been focused outside ourselves, so by the time we got to California I was run down and very sick. We now had a chance to become more inner-directed, and almost immediately issues that we hadn't been aware of began to surface. Our son Daegan wrote an essay shortly after he got to his new school, in which he said his family had recently moved from Washington, D.C. He described each of us as red dots in the midst of a beautiful nature scene, and said that the red dots were slowly turning green. It was true. That was my experience exactly. We were living in a beautiful natural setting, and the ocean and trees were healing us all. We slowed down and became so much more relaxed. Once our minds quieted down, we could see we had been living with an "us and them" mind-set for years, and this perspective had created an enormous imbalance in our inner lives and in our relationship with each other.

DANNY: We realized that we had had an adversarial, confrontational worldview. We had been in the belly of the beast twenty-four/seven, trying to expose the darkest crimes and secrets of the U.S. covert operations community. We knew we couldn't go beyond the "us and them" paradigm without a consciousness shift that generated positive alternative solutions.

It wasn't about giving up on our commitment; it was about coming up with other, creative means of bringing more integrity into the world. It wasn't about winning or losing, about victory or defeat. It was about affirming the positive principles that we believed in and living them, embodying them in our relationships, our work, and our lives.

In our close-knit family, we've experienced surrendering the ego again and again. For me, a trial lawyer, letting go of my will to dominate hasn't been particularly easy. But the evidence that it works has been overwhelming. Learning to sit in a circle and listen openly to each person, and to appreciate different points of view, has been an awakening for us all. In the end, the circle comes up with insights that are far greater than the sum of its parts.

It's not the presence of stress that breaks up couples; it's the absence of love

SARA: And in the space that opens up in the surrender of control is the love we share as a couple and a family. And it's this love that has always gotten us through our challenges and ordeals. Our sex life has always been one of the things we can count on to consistently affirm and strengthen our love. Even in the worst of times, we never let it become a battlefield or a place to act out our differences. Our faithfulness to one another meant that we were always on safe ground together in our physical intimacy. This has been a tremendous blessing and gift to one another. We're a great team, and we have grown together in physical intimacy, emotional support, and mental understanding, but our greatest advances have been in what I call "soul-to-soul loving contact" or "soul connection."

DANNY: We came to trust that the challenges we were given were exactly what we needed in order to move into this next stage of our lives. We have come to understand that the bigger the challenge, the bigger the lesson. Each challenge prepares us for the next step. I'm certain that the reason we are in as good a shape as we are is because our operating principle is love. As long as we stay in that frequency, it may take a while, it may be confusing, but we always find our way.

SARA: We've chosen not to push anything away. In my recent bout with breast cancer, and then just a few months later, colon cancer, this choice has been enormously healing for me. Cancer is a huge lesson in letting go and getting clear about your true priorities. The first week, when I was diagnosed, I reflected on whether I wanted to live. After a week, the will to live rose up inside me more powerfully than I had ever imagined it could, and I got to work. I started doing research on the web, reading books, and changing my lifestyle. I changed my diet and lost a lot of weight. What's important to me now is my growing closeness to God and to those I love, and the unfolding of my soul's service in the world.

Going through the stress that we have can break up families. It can make them crazy and cause them to resent and blame one another. We've been there, done that, and come out the other side because we kept returning to the principle of love.

DANNY: I have been trained, practically from birth, to never give up and to never lose. It's in my cells. These traits can be difficult in family dynamics. It's been my love for Sara and the boys that has allowed me to become more receptive and open. The choice of mate affects your entire life. It's more important than anything else, including your career choice. It affects how you parent your children and the way that life's possibilities show up to you.

Sara and I together are vastly more than either of us could be individually, and we're both always aware of that. We never forget how enriched our lives are by each other. Whether she and I have another year together or another forty years, my life has already been more enriched by her than I could ever have imagined possible.

SARA: One way I show my love to Danny is by doing what I can to promote my healing and to maintain a positive perspective in my life. He has been a prince since I've had cancer, so unbelievably supportive. When I had surgery, he spent the entire week in the hospital room in a chair next to my bed. His presence continually reminds me not to worry. I am fortunate to be with him, and my appreciation of Danny grows stronger all the time.

DANNY: I have only positive thoughts about Sara's healing and recovery, yet I also know that if one of us dies today, I have no regrets. I have no dread of death because I am, and have been, completely happy with Sara and very satisfied with my life. To me, being with Sara every day and every night is as good as it gets. Whatever does or does not lie before us, I've already experienced the awakening of my heart.

3.

A MARRIAGE MAY HAVE TO DIE IN ITS PRESENT FORM TO BE BORN INTO ITS FULL GLORY

Maya and Barry Spector

Many couples know from experience how easy it is to become trapped in their roles while maintaining and providing for a family. The symptoms of such entrapment include feelings of disconnection, emptiness, loneliness, resentment, and ultimately apathy and despair. Without a change in their approach, the only possible outcomes for a trapped couple are divorce or a dead marriage. Barry and Maya had neglected their relationship for years and had drifted into patterns of complacency. By the time they awakened to the consequence of their negligence, it was too late to simply reverse it. But theirs is a story of how, even in the face of what can appear to be a hopelessly broken relationship, the embers of love can continue to burn. Paradoxically, the burial of the old marriage may be required in order for a new relationship to emerge.

There are times when it may be necessary to let go of one's identity as a partner in a couple to recognize the work each individual must do for himself or herself to become more whole. Barry and Maya did not separate with the intention of reuniting. They didn't do their work in order to repair their relationship. Their motivation was much more personal. Each wanted to heal — to become whole and self-reliant and free of crippling codependence. In the process of doing their own work, both became more capable of creating and sustaining the kind of marriage that previously was not possible for them. Their story reveals the work that enabled them to grow into wholeness and shows the commitment required to fulfill this challenge. Barry and Maya embraced their commitment as though their lives depended on it. Ironically, not until something became more compelling than the continuation of their marriage were they finally able to have the relationship they really wanted.

MAYA: I came to Boston in 1970 as a graduate student in library science. I needed to find cheap housing, so I decided to live in a communal household. I answered an ad in the local alternative paper for a space in a household called "the Zoo." That was where I met Barry.

BARRY: I was starting my senior year at Harvard with no plans after graduation. I really didn't have much direction, and I spent most of my time smoking pot and hanging out on the front stoop of the house watching the urban comedy on the street.

MAYA: There was definitely some chemistry between us early on, but it wasn't what you'd call electric. We just found ourselves getting more comfortable with each other and spending more time together.

BARRY: We both discovered yoga, and we became involved with a group in which there was some not-so-subtle pressure from the leadership to fulfill their expectation of what they considered respectability. At this point we had been together for a couple of years, and although we weren't at the time planning to get married, we expected to stay together. The idea of making our relationship legitimate seemed like a pretty natural thing to do, so we did. That was in 1972.

MAYA: Overall, we were happy together during the early years of our relationship. Barry and I had a lot of shared interests, and we supported each other as we cleaned up our lives by making yoga and meditation, rather than pot smoking, our central focus. I worked for about a year as a librarian, and then we both quit our jobs to travel the country. In 1973, we landed in California, and we lived at an ashram in Los Altos for two years. We were spending about five hours a day in meditation and had chosen to be celibate, since the ashram didn't support sexual relationships.

BARRY: It became increasingly clear to us both that something was missing from our lives that the community was not fulfilling. And our disillusionment eventually led to our leaving the group.

MAYA: We left the ashram and lived with friends in Palo Alto. Our sexual relationship resumed, and our first son, Max, was born.

BARRY: I realized that our family needed a consistent source of income, so I started a moving company that quickly became moderately successful. I was caught up in growing and maintaining the business, and Maya was managing the family — we were both busy doing the responsible thing. There was just one problem: our relationship had begun to wither on the vine. With the diminishment of our connection, the juice was drying up, and we gradually, increasingly, found ourselves drifting apart. I wasn't particularly distressed about our growing disconnection — I just saw it as something that couples inevitably go through. But Maya made it clear that she was not okay with it.

You have to be somebody before you can be nobody

MAYA: The loss of our connection disturbed me. I didn't try to conceal my feelings from Barry, but at the same time, neither of us really knew what to do about it. In retrospect, I see that the years we spent trying to obliterate our egos would have been much better spent building a sense of who each of us really was. It's no wonder that our relationship felt empty: neither of us had done much to develop a distinct identity. We had been so busy trying to transcend our egos that we had lost touch with ourselves. It was like going a long way up the wrong road only to reach a dead end, and having to retrace our steps.

BARRY: In the meantime, we had a family and all the responsibilities inherent in that package. Our second son, Alex, was born in 1980, and we continued to throw ourselves completely into meeting the responsibilities of family and business. I was feeling more and more shut down emotionally, with no real understanding of why or what to do about it. I had no outlet for creative expression, which had always been important to me.

MAYA: Neither of us understood at the time just how much care and attention relationships require. We had seriously neglected ours for a long time while attending to other commitments. For me, it was always the kids who occupied my attention. The more Barry and I neglected our relationship, the more prone we were to having small arguments. Our fights weren't especially volatile, but we rarely came through them to a place of real intimacy with each other. We had become companions, not lovers. Things had flattened out, and although our fights weren't intense, neither was anything else in our marriage. No big passions, no big enthusiasms. I got my satisfaction from my kids, my friends, and my personal explorations. I saw that I was experiencing a midlife crisis, and it felt like a slow slide to death.

I had been loyal since day one. I'd committed myself to the family and devoted myself to Barry and the boys. The problem was that I forgot to commit to myself. After almost twenty years of taking care of everyone else's needs, I finally awoke to the toll that self-neglect had taken. I was tired, burnt out, and empty. I was also extremely vulnerable to having an affair, since I was so hungry for a deep emotional connection. In 1990, I met a man named Rick and felt an instant, powerful attraction. When Rick stepped into my life, I felt fully alive for the first time in years. He lit me up, or rather I felt lit up when we were together. It was like coming back from the dead. I didn't want to end my marriage with Barry; I just wanted to join the living again.

Once I did, there was no way I could give that feeling up. But following my heart wasn't easy. Although I no longer felt "in love" with Barry, I still cared for him and felt a strong but conflicted desire to continue to honor my commitment to the marriage. I felt like I was going out of my mind. I was tortured. I was living with one man and totally emotionally involved with another, and it was like being ripped apart. I told Barry what was going on — we'd always been honest with each other, and that wasn't going to change.

BARRY: I was devastated. And I was totally opposed to breaking up. I couldn't understand why we couldn't work things out. I knew Maya needed to find her life again, but I didn't see why we couldn't stay married while she did that. I was willing to do anything to help her retrieve her soul. God knows we were both in excruciating pain.

MAYA: I was convinced I couldn't continue living in what felt like a dead marriage that was killing me. We got into counseling; Barry was hoping that somehow a miracle would save the marriage. I thought it was at best a very long shot but decided to give it a try anyway. After working with the marriage counselor for a year, I announced to Barry that I was leaving. Although I offered to continue to maintain a friendship, Barry was too angry and hurt to agree to that. I moved into a small apartment and, for the first time in my life, had the experience of living alone half the time.

Taking care of yourself may be the best thing you can do for your relationship

MAYA: Shortly after the separation, Rick and I broke up. At first I was upset and scared about losing Rick, but it soon became apparent that staying with him would have been another way of prolonging my old pattern of emotional dependency. I knew that if I was going to be free, I would have to be on my own. I couldn't be with Barry or Rick or any man. If I were with a man, I would just slip back into my old patterns, so I promised myself I would not enter another relationship until I was confident I would never lose myself like that again. I kept my promise, and it would be nearly four years before I was again intimate with a man.

Although I lived alone during that time, I was far from isolated. In those four years, I learned to enjoy my own company and was profoundly nourished by my connections with my friends. My friends understood what I needed and what I was going through, and they knew how to be with me. I was learning things like setting boundaries, saying "no," and telling the truth. I had been a people-pleaser my whole life, and I knew that, until I recovered from this, I'd never have a healthy relationship. I got something from my friends that I never got from therapy: I began to understand that Barry, even though he loved me, could never give me, me. I got myself back.

BARRY: Not only were we physically separated, but I severed our emotional ties too. We had practically no interaction or communication with each other — we spoke only when we had to work out arrangements for the boys — and our divorce became final one year after the separation. The separation ignited a process in me similar to Maya's. I reacted to these unwanted changes in my life with a combination of grief, anxiety, and rage; I went from being shut down and depressed to being wildly emotional. My moods were spinning all over the place. I had fought the breakup for months, and when it finally happened all hell broke loose inside me. I loved and needed Maya, but at the same time I hated her for leaving me, for not hanging in there to make the marriage work. But I also understood her need to save herself. In retrospect it was exactly what we both needed. We were both dying inside that marriage. The difference between us was that she knew it and I didn't. I'm incredibly grateful to Maya today for what she did. She saved both our lives.

I began seeing a psychologist, who helped me climb out of my grief. With Maya no longer filling the emptiness in my life, I was motivated to turn to others, mostly my men friends, for support. In addition, a bodyworker helped me release a lot of old emotional wounds lodged in my muscles and tissues, and I joined a weekly men's group. Through all that work, I came to see that it wasn't a simple matter in which Maya was the villain and I was the victim. We'd both played a part in the breakdown of our marriage and the deadness of our individual lives. My friends helped me see my complicity in things. They didn't just sympathize with me and demonize Maya.

Love is the bridge between anger and respect

BARRY: After four years of separation, we attended a powerful personal growth workshop. There were several hundred people in the auditorium, and I sat as far away from Maya as I could get, but was intensely aware of her the entire day. At the dinner break, I felt prompted to act spontaneously, and I found myself telling her we had to go to dinner together. I began our dinner conversation by saying, "I want to thank you for divorcing me. I was shut down and out of touch with my feelings, way more out of touch than I'd realized at the time. I was missing so much but had no idea what I was missing. I have come to understand that it's never one person who is completely responsible for causing a divorce, and I acknowledge the part I played in the breakdown of our marriage. I realize now that, if you hadn't done what you did, I never would have gone through what I did in order to develop and heal myself. Nothing short of losing you in divorce would have rocked my world enough to propel me into the life I now have. And I wouldn't trade this life for anything. Thank you."

MAYA: I just sat in silence as Barry spoke. I was stunned to see and hear the transformation in him. That evening was the first time in over four years that the two of us had had a personal conversation. Over the next few weeks, we gradually made more contact, tentatively at first and then with more ease. Then one day, I got a call from Barry informing me that our son Max had totaled his car and was injured, though not critically. I rushed over to the house just as the tow truck was bringing the mangled vehicle into the driveway. When I saw the smashed car and realized how close we had come to losing our son, I burst into tears and fell sobbing into Barry's arms. He was right there for me. He was with me for the first time in many, many years.

BARRY: Max's accident proved to be a pivotal experience in our new relationship. It brought us back together and helped us to more fully open our hearts to each other. We began spending more time together and, for the first time in years, finding some openness in each other's company. Alongside the pleasure, joy, and delight was a fear that we might be opening ourselves up to disappointment and once again experience the trauma of divorce. We lived together for eight years, and then one day, for the second time in my life, I popped the question to Maya. We really didn't need to get married again. We could have just continued to live blended lives without the benefit of a marriage license, but somehow it felt right, and we both agreed it was what we wanted.

Marriage vows are sacred words with transformative power

MAYA: This time around we put a great deal of time and care into the preparations for our wedding. We cowrote the entire ceremony and wrote and recited poetry to each other. The wedding took place on the thirty-first anniversary of the day we met. We proclaimed that the guiding purpose of our union was to express our individual purposes and support each other in their fulfillment. We pledged to live more consciously, with open hearts.

BARRY: Neither of us was willing to be half of the Barry and Maya package. I committed to maintaining my close ties with my men friends, and I have. Now, Maya doesn't have the burden of being my only strong emotional support. We also vowed to have at least one getaway every month in order to deepen the quality of intimacy in our relationship. We've hardly missed a month yet.

MAYA: Our life is so good now. At times it's still kind of hard to believe. We've come so far and come through so much. But we've both done a lot of work to get to this point. Nobody handed us this experience. We earned it.

BARRY: We know that, as good as things are, they can always be better. There's too much at stake to go back to sleep.

4.

IT'S ALWAYS POSSIBLE TO MAKE TIME FOR YOUR MARRIAGE, EVEN IF YOU HAVE TWELVE KIDS

Rachel and Nehemia Cohen (not their real names)

When we left the home of Rachel and Nehemia Cohen after our first interview with them, we agreed that we would never again complain that we were too busy to do something. And nearly two years later, we've kept our word. Nehemia, or Rabbi Nehemia as he is known to his congregation, and his wife, Rachel, give new meaning to the metaphor of having a lot on your plate. As the parents of twelve children ages five to twenty-five, they have personal and social responsibilities and commitments greater than the average couple can even begin to imagine.

Rabbi Cohen is more than the spiritual leader of his congregation: he is viewed by his community as a source of guidance, wisdom, and help to all who call on him. As a longtime member of the Chabad movement, the rabbi has committed his life to service. His Chabad center serves more than twelve thousand people a year.

Our first encounter with the Cohens was at their home, where we were treated, along with a dozen other guests, to the kind of sumptuous feast they partake in each week to mark the beginning of the Sabbath. At one point the rabbi sang a song of gratitude and appreciation to his beloved Rachel while we looked on, moved beyond words.

Nehemia and Rachel claim that the source of their seemingly boundless energy comes not from themselves or each other but from the intensity of their spiritual connection. As they assured us during our talks together, there is no separating their spiritual connection from their love for each other. Together Rachel and Nehemia stand as living proof that, when something is important enough, we can somehow manage to find time for it, even when there are fourteen mouths to feed.

NEHEMIA: Rachel and I were both brought up in the Brooklyn Heights section of New York City, in the midst of a deeply Hassidic lifestyle. At the time that I met her, I was teaching. We both grew up with a reverence for the teachings of Rabbi Menachem Mendel Schneerson, whom we all called "the Rebbe." He was a spiritual guide who formed the identity of thousands. His teachings started the Chabad movement, which sends people all over the world to bring Jews back to Judaism.

RACHEL: We were brought up in the same kind of religious home. Both our fathers were rabbis, and before we even met each other we knew we would choose to marry someone committed to living a life of service. When we met I was only twenty, but I was clear about what I was looking for in a husband. I knew I didn't want a businessman or someone else whose primary focus in life was making money. I was looking for a man dedicated to spirituality and service. By the time we had our second date, I knew Nehemia was the one for me, but he needed one more date to be sure. After six weeks, we decided to get married.

Great marriages require a commitment to something beyond the relationship itself

NEHEMIA: In our tradition, there is not only no sex before marriage but also no physical contact of any kind: no kissing or hugging or even touching. The purpose is to make sure that the bond is not based on physical attraction alone, or even primarily. It's a hard discipline, but our overriding commitment has always been to serve God, so we honor the teachings.

RACHEL: It's hard to follow the strict rules, but I was committed to building a holy home. I wanted to do everything possible to start on the right foot. Our marriage started on a strong foundation.

NEHEMIA: We have had a purpose for our relationship from the very beginning, and our alignment with this purpose has given rise to a great marriage.

We are not one of those couples who believe that, to be successful, we have to focus on each other. Our marriage is based on a shared goal, a home for our children and grandchildren, and contribution to our community. If the marriage is too focused on the self, it can be too small and make the people involved selfish. If you feel called to a higher purpose, you do what is commanded, rather than choosing what you want. There is a strong theme running through our family: because we recognize a higher purpose, we have a commitment to responsibility that allows us to do things even when we don't always want to.

RACHEL: We both grew up understanding the meaning of sacrifice. We made the decision together that we wanted to work for Chabad.

NEHEMIA: When we arrived in our new community, it required a tremendous amount of outreach. I wasn't sure exactly what to do, so I just got out the phone book and started calling people with Jewish names and inviting them to a service. We have a synagogue, but there is no formal membership as in a typical synagogue. Ninety percent of the work I do is outside the synagogue. We open our home on Friday night for Shabbat dinner. Our policy is that you can't be invited, because you're always invited.

RACHEL: It's typical for us to have fifteen people at Shabbat dinner. The kids don't like it when we don't have a bunch of guests. Having so many children makes it difficult for Nehemia and me to have time to be alone with each other. It's almost impossible for us to vacation together. I find that, from time to time, I'm annoyed that he has to go to work early in the morning — because he conducts services every day at 6:30 AM — and then has late-evening appointments on top of his full day. But it is much easier to clear the annoyance because I know he is doing good works. He's not just playing golf. If he calls to say something has come up and he'll be home later than expected, I find it easier to get over my disappointment because I trust that it must be important. I know that, if I really needed him, Nehemia would drop everything he's doing to be with me. Last week, I had surgery on both feet. Nehemia took off most of the week to be home to take care of me and the children.

NEHEMIA: We believe in having a balanced life. If you love your work, that's great. But if you make your job everything, you're in trouble. Last week, one of the members of the congregation said, "Your public needs you." I said, "My public needs to see that I am home with my wife who just had surgery." My secretaries all know that when I say I'm not taking any calls, what that really means is that I'm not taking calls from anyone except my wife.

Service isn't what you do; it's the generosity of spirit that informs your actions

NEHEMIA: I see my marriage as being a lot like a mountain I climbed in Israel. I wanted very badly to visit the grave of a famous rabbi I admired, but to reach the holy teacher's grave I had to climb the mountain on a very hot day. It was far to climb in the heat, but when I stopped on one of the switchbacks and looked out and saw how far I had come, it gave me strength to keep going. I would take one step and then one step more. Like climbing the mountain, our growth in our marriage has been a step at a time.

RACHEL: We have so many rituals that support us. Although my husband sings a song to me every Friday night, he is not just singing to me personally; it is so much bigger than that. He is singing in praise of the virtues of all Jewish women and the divine feminine. The theme of the song is a woman of valor. Every day we say a psalm together, and we bless each other with our actions. On Friday nights and holidays, we light a candle for each of the children and pray for their well-being, and every day we spend time thinking about our children's education.

NEHEMIA: There are many ups and downs in marriage. There are times when negativity can threaten to overtake our minds. But I have seen some of the most broken-down marriages come back together once couples have a change in their thinking. Once couples begin to look at each other as their best friend, close the back door, and choose to recommit to the marriage, amazing transformations can occur. When people lose the path, they sometimes need help from family, friends, or a spiritual advisor to find what has meaning in their lives. Together they can make a commitment to keep going forward. Rachel and I continually recommit to that which we hold as sacred, to each other, to our children, and to service in our community.

RACHEL: Our spiritual life is our family and our service to our community. If you are climbing up a mountain carrying a heavy load in a backpack that you believe is filled with stones, you will feel differently than if you are carrying a backpack you know is full of diamonds. For me, having twelve children is the backpack full of diamonds. It's a lot of responsibility, of course, and a lot of work, but it's what I choose and what I love.

NEHEMIA: A man once said to me about having so many children: "How can you do this to your wife?"

RACHEL: That man thought I was a powerless rabbi's wife. He didn't have an accurate picture of how Hassidic men treat their wives. Nehemia and I are in this life and this work together, and all our major decisions are made together. I can disagree, and I sometimes do. I can make choices that Nehemia disapproves of, which I sometimes do. I am very much my own person.

When you view others with respect, they often rise to the level of your estimation

NEHEMIA: I ask Rachel's advice about everything I undertake. I follow it, because I know from years of experience that her advice is golden 99 percent of the time. I also have a very capable advisory board at my disposal. Chabad is everywhere, all over the world. I have an email list of 950 rabbis that I consult with often, but the best advice I get always comes from my wife.

RACHEL: Sharing power and authority has never been a big challenge
for us. We have very similar attitudes and beliefs that have served us
well. I do the rituals of housework as an offering to God. In New York,
where we grew up with the teachings of the wisest rabbis and their
wives to guide us, we learned that children are the greatest of all
the great blessings. I was so happy and eager to have children. The difficult part has been being in the midst of a more secular culture that
doesn't share our values. It's also a big challenge to find time to be together, in the face of the children's and the community's needs. It is
hard to raise children properly in this world, with plenty of time and attention devoted to each one. We have come to appreciate that raising
children is the greatest blessing that life has to offer.

NEHEMIA: Financial security has been one of our challenges over the
years. We have lived through many times when we didn't know where
the next penny was coming from. Having so many children and doing
service has required both of us to have great faith. We had to stop worrying and get out there to do our work, and trust that the divine would
provide for us. Our faith just keeps getting deeper and deeper in response to our life experience.

RACHEL: We know better than to think we are the ones causing the
results. We are not in charge. There is a mighty force taking care of
things, and we have great peace of mind knowing that we only have to
do our part, and that we can turn over the rest.

5.

THERE ARE THOUSANDS OF WAYS TO MAKE LOVE

Judith Sherven and Jim Sniechowski

Judith was forty-three and never married when she met Jim. She was, however, experienced in dating . . . and dating and dating. She would tell her friends: "I would do well in marriage if I could only get in one." Having been a clinical psychologist for twenty years, she had consulted with hundreds of singles and couples, helping them to more effectively deal with the challenges of their relationships.

At the time of their meeting, Jim was forty-five, had a PhD in human behavior, and had two marriages under his belt. A veteran of many relationships himself, he was seeking to create one that would last. At the time, Jim was Mr. Laid-Back. He read and wrote poetry, and though he was successful, he hated his job as an investment banker. Judith was compulsive and controlled, loved to travel, and had a thriving private psychotherapy practice.

A year after meeting, they married with the shared intention to discover the key to a successful relationship, not only for their own sake but for the benefit of others as well. To their surprise, and their joy, they discovered it wasn't necessary to compromise themselves to have a fulfilling marriage. In fact, they saw that maintaining a separate self is as essential in a relationship as care and concern for one's partner.

They also came to recognize the many differences between them that required their attention. Jim and Judith are two very powerful personalities, and at times heated arguments erupted. In honoring their commitment to learning and becoming more conscious, each has adopted some of the best qualities of the other without losing his or her unique identity. Jim has become much more organized and more visionary in his work. Judith has become more easygoing and trusting of her rational and intuitive wisdom. "We have," says Judith, "fertilized one another's world by our differences."

Conventional wisdom dictates that a successful marriage requires both partners to make the relationship their highest priority. Jim and Judith, like many other couples in our book, have subordinated their commitment to their relationship to a higher commitment. Their shared commitment is to become more conscious, aware, and authentic, not just in their marriage, but also in their lives in general, and to use their relationship as a vehicle to support this process. Not surprisingly, their intention has been tested many times. The first and most challenging test came at the very beginning, on their honeymoon in Paris. Within hours of their wedding, the couple experienced a breakdown that could have become a deal breaker, but which ultimately proved far more valuable than they could possibly have anticipated. Their rough start proved to be the source of some of the very lessons they needed in order to turn their vision into a reality.

Your track record isn't necessarily an accurate predictor of your future

JIM: Judith and I met on a blind date. We were both in our forties. I had two divorces behind me, and Judith had never been married. We were living in Los Angeles and enjoying successful careers — at the time I was working as an investment banker, and Judith was in her eleventh year of private practice as a clinical psychologist.

JUDITH: Looking back it was clear that I was consumed by the Prince Charming myth. I've always had a tendency toward perfectionism, and I was looking for "Mr. Perfect." It took me a while to realize he didn't exist. When I met Jim, I wasn't swept off my feet, but there was clearly something there between us. I am business-focused, upfront, earthbound, bottom-line driven, and obsessive.

JIM: And cover-girl beautiful and the love of my life. I am mellow, laid-back, emotional, intuitive, poetic, and imaginative. We are highly distinctive individuals with very different personalities. One thing we both agree on, though, is that our differences are the source of our greatest joys and accomplishments, as well as the source of our most difficult challenges. We are also convinced that it was not our individual differences in our previous relationships that broke them but our failure to appreciate and work with those differences.

JUDITH: We each had a strong desire to create a long-term relationship and, by the time we met, had come to realize that, no matter who we partnered with, unless we learned to appreciate differences, our future would be no different from our past. Shortly after meeting, we both recognized that we were with our life partners. But rather than jumping into marriage, we agreed to first build our friendship and then conduct our courtship slowly and consciously.

The commitment is to the process, not the marriage

JIM: Our commitment was not to each other, or even to the relationship, but to the process of becoming more conscious and more aware. To support this process, we spent vast amounts of time engaged in conversations designed to help clarify and reveal our deepest feelings, desires, and values. We committed to being ourselves completely, and to risking being authentic with each other, even if it meant losing the relationship. After all, we knew there was no way it would work if we were not authentic with each other, and that if we were, there was at least a good chance it might work.

JUDITH: As our connection deepened, we shared our concerns and hopes about marriage and designed our own prenuptial agreement that would serve as a guide for marriage. We each pledged to make the well-being of our relationship a higher priority than our individual preferences. We also agreed to honor our differences rather than try to homogenize them. Even though we were not exactly sure what this would entail, we were committed to learning how to do it, confident that, with mutual support, we would be successful. Our wedding took place exactly one year after we met. Our vows, which we wrote ourselves, specifically referred to our commitment to honor our differences.

JIM: We put a great deal of special attention into planning every detail of our wedding and honeymoon. We agreed that Paris would be the perfect honeymoon destination. But before we even arrived there, our carefully planned, ideal honeymoon became a nightmare. We had rented a car and were driving into Paris. I was at the wheel and, having never driven there, didn't know my way around. It took every ounce of my concentration to deal with the traffic and the driving style of Parisians, which was different from anything I had encountered before. I was tense, trying not to get into an accident or get hopelessly lost. Suddenly Judith let out a bloodcurdling scream that made the hairs on the back of my neck stand on end. I was sure that, at the very least, a huge semi was bearing down on us and we were about to meet our deaths. When Judith finally found words, she screamed, "I left my nightgown in the hotel!" Well, I flew into an absolute rage when I realized what a big deal she was making out of something I saw as insignificant. It was just a piece of cloth that could easily be replaced.

JUDITH: It was much more than a piece of cloth to me. It was a symbol of our love and marriage. It represented the beginning of our legal and public commitment to share our lives together. How could he not understand how precious my honeymoon nightgown was? Jim's reaction to my outburst sent me into a tailspin. I was devastated.

JIM: I was enraged and, at the same time, felt horrible that this situation was destroying our dream of a perfect honeymoon. We hadn't even made it to Paris, and already it seemed to be trashed. We couldn't get out of an emotional loop: I kept raging and Judith kept sobbing. She was upset with herself for ruining everything, and I felt like I was trapped with a crazy woman. Although I was committed to the marriage and knew I loved Judith and was not going to leave her, I was not feeling optimistic about our future. I was thinking, "Shit, I guess this piece comes with her too!" This was not part of my fantasy of what we would have together.

JUDITH: By around eleven that night we were thoroughly exhausted and hungry, since we hadn't eaten for more than ten hours. We agreed to stop fighting long enough to get something to eat, hoping it might help. It did. We were able to finally hear each other. Over the meal, we slowly and guardedly admitted that we had been out of line. In becoming more vulnerable and exposing our deeper feelings, we uncovered hidden pain and fear that we were carrying. The incident had activated very old, raw wounds for us both. It brought back memories of my father raging when he didn't get what he wanted, and my terror of his anger and the feeling that I couldn't do anything right.

JIM: For me, it awakened memory of an experience I often had as a child, of not being seen for who I am. I was under a lot of stress, really on edge. It was inconceivable to me that Judith couldn't understand where I was. Once again, I felt unseen, misunderstood, unacknowledged. I felt justified in my rage and wanted an apology from Judith. At the same time, another part of me was asking, "What is my part in this breakdown?" I knew it wasn't all her, and I found myself feeling guilty and avoiding her eyes.

Both sides were real and valid. Somehow, I had to let the part of me that wanted to connect with Judith overcome the part of me that wanted to be right. I began thinking about the vows we had so recently made, and this helped me strengthen my commitment to let down my defenses and open up to Judith. We had vowed never to walk away from a conflict, but to resolve it no matter how long it took. We were clearly being put to the test now.

JUDITH: Slowly, we recognized that we were both experiencing some version of "I don't know who you are right now, but I know that I love you. I just can't see you very clearly because my own pain is in the way." We reached across the table to take each other's hands. We were both crying. I felt my heart soften, and I dropped into a much deeper level of vulnerability. I explained to Jim that his rage had brought me back to a horrid memory of being a little girl sitting at a Thanksgiving dinner table surrounded by anger, animosity, tension, and unhappiness. My pain and terror at the time had been unbearable. To keep my sanity, I had focused obsessively on the dishes and place settings. When Jim indicated that he understood the importance that simple objects had for me, I began to feel less alone.

JIM: As things cooled down between us, I became aware of what had triggered my response to Judith. As she shifted her focus away from me and began talking about her own feelings and experiences, I felt myself relax and soften. I began to understand, while she was pouring out her childhood pain, that the missing nightgown was more than an article of clothing: it was a sacred vestment and a source of refuge for her. For Judith, physical things can have a special meaning that they don't generally have for me.

Almost simultaneously, I began to see why I had reacted to her as strongly as I had. Judith's inability to appreciate my concerns about our safety in what had felt like a dangerous situation had kicked up some strong feelings about not having been taken seriously by my father when I was a kid. I worshiped my dad when I was small, and once again I felt powerless to connect to someone whose attention I desperately needed at the moment.

We both had been blinded by nearly overwhelming feelings, and until things began to cool down it had been impossible for either of us to connect to the other. As we talked that night, our wedding vows came back to me and I reminded myself that I had loved Judith yesterday, that I would love her tomorrow, and that this disconnect was only temporary. I also became powerfully aware that, in any conflict, both sides bring a piece of truth to the picture.

Our similarities bring us comfort and safety; our differences ignite our passion and prompt our deepest growth

JUDITH: The fight in Paris was the worst we've ever had in all our years together. It's possible that we never experienced anything remotely that horrible again because we learned so much from the experience. One of the big lessons for me was to recognize and own my fear when it's triggered, and not act it out. I've learned to manage my feelings rather than blurt out something in the heat of the moment. There's a difference between respectfully expressing my deeper feelings and indulging the impulse to dump my anger, which always has negative consequences. Jim and I have also learned that the sources of our fights are never really what we're arguing about. It's not until we get to a deeper level of our feelings that we stop the cycle of blame-and-defend and explore what the drama is really about.

JIM: Working with our differences has become a central theme for us. We are both convinced that the differences between people are the basis for the deepest intimacy. When we are respected for being different, we feel loved for who we really are. The differences themselves, and skillfully addressing them, bring magic to a relationship. We know there is wisdom in the choice we made, that we were drawn to each other because of the ways we are different, not despite them.

JUDITH: As we've learned to appreciate rather than judge our differences, we've learned to love them and love each other more. Our differences have motivated us to come up with all kinds of creative ways to show love and make love.

It's possible to have sex without making love, and to make love without having sex

JIM: You can make love anywhere, any time, and we do! I'm not talking about having sex, which is what most people mean when they use the phrase. Of course, sex can be a wonderful form of lovemaking, a real expression of your love for each other. But lovemaking doesn't have to be limited to sex. In fact, one of the things that can diminish the depth of feeling in a marriage is the failure to use nonsexual means of expression to show appreciation and connect with each other.

Early on in our relationship, we decided to see how creative we could be in expressing and sharing our love. When we redefined love-making, we began coming up with all kinds of ways to enjoy and celebrate our connection with each other. We both find sex very plea-surable, but it's only one manifestation of lovemaking out of an infinite variety of forms.

JUDITH: Lovemaking is about mutual affection and care. You make love whenever you recognize and respect, and really appreciate, your partner for who he or she is. When we actively seek out creative ways to please each other, to bring more joy into each other's lives, we are making love. When we do this for each other, we create a positive flow that then extends to others.

For example, Jim loves dogs. I'm not that into dogs, but since they are special to him I buy him cards with dogs on them. I found a pencil with a doggie eraser, a dog refrigerator magnet, even a Kleenex box with dogs on it. When I give him things like these, it means, "I see who you are and what is important to you, and I honor you." Lovemaking is affection, care, and playfulness.

JIM: Judith's mind works differently from mine. She has a lot of trou-ble relating to the computer, for example. I thought she was having tantrums at first, and it was annoying, but then I understood that her mind simply works differently. Now when she has a problem with the computer, I contain my impatience and solve the problem with her. We are making love when I recognize and appreciate Judith for herself, not as a projection of who I want her to be. Then she feels really loved.

JUDITH: I love Valentine's Day, but Jim doesn't. Last Valentine's Day, he made seven Valentine cards with stickers and his own poetry on each card. Every day for a week leading up to Valentine's Day, he placed a card somewhere I would find it. I got one propped up on the toilet, with the seat down, of course. There was one on my computer when I came home from grocery shopping. Another appeared on my pillow one evening. The whole thing cost three dollars, but it meant so much to me that I am going to frame them. His gift and my receiving it, that's making love.

JIM: Listening, admiring, respecting, and showing care are all ways of making love. But, just as important, is the kind of lovemaking that occurs when you're willing to confront. When I see Judith doing something that I know will hurt her in some way, I'm willing to risk saying so. Because she's sensitive to sugar, for example, if she's about to order pastry or ice cream for dessert I might ask, "Do you really want that?"

JUDITH: My ability to graciously receive Jim's feedback is a way that I make love with him. I know he's not only my spouse but also my ally. I need his feedback, and he needs mine, if we are to grow into the best we can be. Because I really trust Jim's love for me, I receive his feedback as support and I appreciate it rather than feel criticized by it. I trust that he always wants the best for me, as do I for him.

Jim is an outdoor person and very close to nature. Since I grew up in the city, I missed out on some of the natural beauty of nature. Whenever there are fireflies, he always lets me know so I can enjoy the moment with him. Where we live there are spectacularly beautiful, iridescent, pale-green luna moths with ten-inch wingspans. It's common for Jim to run in yelling, "Judith, you have to see this!" He wants to bring beauty to me, and this is certainly making love.

We've found that the issues that arise in our marriage almost always relate to unresolved issues from our childhoods. When they come up and we address them, they become less prominent in our lives. Our willingness to directly face all that life presents, rather than avoid what is unpleasant, brings us ever-increasing passion and fulfillment. It's why our relationship just keeps getting better and better.

6.

A TRUE PARTNERSHIP AMPLIFIES THE JOY OF SUCCESS AND DIMINISHES THE PAIN OF DISTRESS

Jim Brochu and Steve Schalchlin

Five days after meeting on a cruise ship in 1985, Steve and Jim agreed to move in together. With the exception of a brief separation in 1996, they've been inseparable ever since. Before they met, neither Steve nor Jim had ever been involved in a long-term committed relationship, and neither had any interest in creating one at the time. All that quickly changed.

What they discovered early on was that both were not only accomplished professional musicians but great collaborators as well. Over the years, Steve and Jim have worked together creating and producing songs, shows, and musical productions that they've performed for audiences throughout the country and internationally. After reading a review of their show *Big Voice: God or Merman* in the *San Francisco Chronicle*, we first made contact with them.

One aspect of their relationship that Steve and Jim most appreciate is the amount of laughter and play (musical and otherwise) they engage in together. It's a cornerstone of their relationship and an integral part of the creativity that fuels their work. Eight years into their relationship, however, the two were faced with a life-threatening challenge that pushed play off the map completely. Practically overnight, Jim became not only a life partner but also a full-time caregiver when Steve's HIV condition exploded into a full-blown case of AIDS. Within a few months Steve's dying was no longer a possibility or likelihood; it was an imminent reality.

There are times when surrendering our resistance to what appears to be inevitable opens up a new possibility, something not previously imagined. Although eventually Steve became too debilitated for either of them to hope for a miracle, a miracle is what they received. And yet the real miracle is not that Steve was rescued from death's door but that these two men learned life lessons during their extended ordeal and have applied those teachings in creative ways since Steve's recovery.

JIM: Steve and I met in 1985 on a cruise. Being a playwright and an actor can sometimes be exhausting, and at the time it was clear to me that I was badly in need of a break. I had come across an ad in a magazine for a five-day cruise to Bermuda for only two hundred dollars. I called a friend, and we both signed up for it. When we got on the boat, it was obvious that, even at that price, they were overcharging! Steve was the ship's piano player, and I was a high-class passenger. We met on the first day of the cruise and spent just about the entire trip talking. We had many interests in common, not just music. We laughed a lot and enjoyed each other enormously. On the fifth day, I said to Steve, "Why don't you come live with me?"

Steve was a bit shocked at my abrupt offer. So I suggested he take the evening to think it over, and said that if he wanted to come with me, he should meet me at lifeboat number six the next morning at eight o'clock. The next morning, I was excited and nervous, and I posted myself next to lifeboat number six. Steve didn't show up. It was just like the *Sleepless in Seattle* scene with Tom Hanks and Meg Ryan missing each other on the top of the Empire State Building. My friend who was on the trip with me found me and said Steve was looking all over the ship for me. When we finally found each other, I was delighted that Steve said he wanted to come live with me.

STEVE: My background is completely different from Jim's. I'm from Arkansas, and my father was a Southern Baptist missionary. My parents were kind, gentle, simple people, and very religious. Jim had been exposed to the world of art and theater from a very early age. I had been playing in bands, so my knowledge was primarily of pop music, and when I got the job on the ship I had to learn the standard songs that people would request. I didn't know theater music or show tunes, so it was a steep learning curve for me the year I lived on the ship.

JIM: I was born and bred in New York, and I come from a traditional musical theater background. My mom died when I was two years old, and my father never remarried. My father and I raised each other. I grew up in Brooklyn, close to Manhattan, and went to the theater every single week. I wanted to be a priest until I was thirteen years old — that was when I saw Ethel Merman in *Gypsy*. It was a life-changing moment; I knew then that I had to be in theater. I've been involved in show business for forty years. The first year Steve and I were together, we lived in very close quarters in a studio apartment. We bought a beautiful weekend place in Pennsylvania as a getaway. Even though I had been out for many years, it was still daunting to move into a new community, particularly one in a conservative area. We didn't know if we would be accepted — we just kept our fingers crossed.

STEVE: There were twenty houses together in an enclave on a private lake, a very conservative enclave. We had been meeting individuals over the first months we lived there, and then one night we threw a big party and invited all the residents of our new community. We knew we were in the right place when they all showed up wearing buttons proclaiming "Jim for Vice President." They wanted Jim to run for the office of vice president of our homeowner's association.

Once we put down some roots and got established in our new home, we started a project together: a musical that we cowrote in the studio I built in the Pennsylvania house. We moved to Los Angeles because Jim had a job opportunity writing for television. I put aside being an artist to become a businessman and took a job running a nonprofit organization that helped young artists get a start in the industry.

Hardship can be the source of great devotion

STEVE: Then in 1993, all that came to an end when my HIV condition became AIDS. I got very sick and was sure I was going to die. My health just kept going downhill, and I was bedridden for over two years. Jim and I celebrated our "lasts." We celebrated what we believed would be our last vacation, our last Christmas, and our last birthdays together. For about a year, I was so weak I couldn't even sit up. I couldn't read a book because my arms were too weak to hold it up.

JIM: Steve was walking death. He's over six feet tall, and his weight dropped to a hundred pounds. He was just skin and bones. It was certain that it was only a matter of time before he'd be gone, and I put everything I had into trying to keep him alive. I let go of everything else. We went into financial ruin because neither of us was working. All our bills were mounting up. We survived by standing in line for free bread, cheese, milk, and other necessities at various AIDS service organizations. We also received a few grants from some music industry groups to help pay for electricity.

Gratitude is always an option
no matter what the circumstances

STEVE: Jim was my twenty-four-hour-a-day nurse. He had to learn to give me shots. It was years of sacrifice, but he never wavered. Jim was unbelievable. He never once laid a trip on me about my prolonged illness being a burden to him. The kind of stress that we were going through is the kind that either pulls couples apart or draws them closer together. For us, fortunately, it was the latter. We became closer than ever. I was inspired to write love songs to Jim in my deep appreciation of his care for me. My songs were about how I felt being so sick, facing death, and how the love of my friends kept me alive. When I was writing the songs, and singing those songs, I felt a lot better. My plan was to write enough songs to have one last concert and then die.

JIM: Then in 1996, a new AIDS medication came on the market. It was expected to be highly effective, but there was just one problem: there was a very limited supply, and not nearly enough for all the AIDS patients who needed it. A lottery was held to determine which patients would receive it, and Steve was one of the lucky winners. Most of those who did not get the drug died. The doctors told us that Steve was about two weeks away from death when he started to take the medication. It was hailed as a revolutionary AIDS drug because everyone who was put on it began to revive. As soon as Steve started to take it, he came back to life.

STEVE: The medication rescued me from death's door; but ironically it was when I got well and felt strong that we had the most difficult time in our relationship.

JIM: The new drug gave Steve a new personality. Shortly after he started taking it, he became aggressive and angry. It was a nightmare. We didn't know at the time that the drug caused his mood changes. Around this time, a third party came into our life, and he noticed that our relationship was not in good shape. He took advantage of our vulnerability, pretending to be a good guy who was trying to keep us together while, behind our backs, he bad-mouthed each of us to the other, trying to split us up. Over a period of six weeks, things went from bad to worse. It got so bad that we had to separate. It just goes to show you that a relationship that had been strong for thirteen years could still be fragile. We learned that if we didn't take care of our relationship all the time, it could rapidly slip into disrepair.

The separation lasted eighty days, and although it was necessary, it was enormously difficult for us both. I stayed in Los Angeles, and Steve moved back to New York. We talked on the phone every day and stayed in touch, but we needed some space to see things clearly.

What doesn't kill a relationship can make it stronger

STEVE: We missed each other terribly and longed to be together again. Finally in one conversation, I said to Jim, "Why don't you come home? Let's just be nice to each other." We made a commitment to be kind and respectful. And we were. We had indulged in speaking too many unkind words to each other. We had hurt each other terribly. It was enough, more than enough. We agreed that we would not bring up old hurts, and we didn't. In time, our deliberate practice of kindness became a habit, and we began to trust enough to discuss what had happened. It wasn't too long before we were laughing at how ridiculously immature we had been.

I got a new doctor who treated the diabetes that was a side effect of my HIV medicine. It took a while to straighten things out, but once I got on the proper medication, I got back my emotional equilibrium. My mood changed back to being more like it had been. It had been a period of temporary madness in which we were both caught up in a storm of overwhelming feelings. Slowly we were able to sort out what had happened, and began to talk about the third party in a responsible way. We each owned up to our part in the breakdown.

That was an unusual time for us. We had always spent a lot of time together and had rarely had even a minor conflict, and never a prolonged one. That painful breakdown was a powerful lesson for us. It showed us that, even when small upsets occur, it can sometimes be a good idea for us to take some separate space and leave the issue aside for a while. Then later on, when we pick the issue up again, we're more relaxed and we can talk about it more productively. Nowadays, we don't waste much energy on power struggles and breakdowns. We've found a way of being together that works. Having such ease in our relationship allows our creative energies to pour forth.

In 2002, a big theater asked us to do a piece together. We wrote the piece thinking we were writing about a religious journey, but the piece kept morphing until it ended up being about our relationship. As we started performing the play, we found ourselves in a theater filled with older Jewish couples who hadn't had much contact with gays. When we stayed around to speak with them after the performance, they said things like "We've learned more about gay couples in the last two hours than we have in our previous lives together. You're really just like us, aren't you?"

JIM: We consider ourselves extremely fortunate. We share a great committed relationship *and* we have work that allows us to travel. But our greatest pleasure is simply to stay home. Our idea of a great vacation is to lock the door to our house for a week and nestle into our separate creative spaces at home. Steve pulls the audience into the pits of hell.

He brings rawness to the story and makes people feel. Then, just when it gets almost too intense, I lighten things up. It's a nice balance. We can deliver a heavy, important message, and the whole experience can still be light and funny. Our reviews attest to that!

STEVE: Even though we work in separate rooms, we are still somehow connected. Jim was able to bring the songs together in a beautiful way. During the rehearsal stage, we always work collaboratively. There is a lot of goodwill and a lot of give and take. We enjoy the process because we trust and respect each other so much. We know that we each get our say, so we always feel free to experiment, to try things out to see if they will work.

JIM: I sometimes need to get out of the house to have some breathing room. We trust each other to take time away for solitude. It's never been a problem. We never take it as a rejection of the other person. We both trust that it will be only a short break, and that we'll be back together soon, usually even better than before. Because we know when to leave each other alone, our home is a place of great ease and peace. I think it's as easy as it is because Steve is such a good soul; he's just a good person. Look at the advocacy work that he did with the young artists. Of course, he can be a pain in the ass sometimes, but he makes me laugh a lot and he likes my cooking. The glue that keeps us together is laughter.

STEVE: Jim has tremendous intelligence and wit, and his personality is off the scale! He is good at keeping my life, and our life together, nice and even. We have perfected the art of leaving each other alone. It may sound overly simple, but I think one of the secrets of our relationship is that we treat each other as adults, and we don't slip into being each other's parent. It's based on the very deep level of respect that we have for each other. That and the humor we bring to each other make it easy for love and appreciation to thrive in our relationship. That glue that Jim said keeps us together just seems to get stronger all the time. Why would either of us ever want to lose something this good?

7.

PAINFUL BREAKDOWNS CONTAIN THE SEEDS NECESSARY FOR LOVE TO FLOURISH

Shirley and Drew Coleman (not their real names)

There can be times in the course of a marriage when one partner believes everything is fine and the other one feels the relationship is slowly dying on the vine. When one partner's grievances, disappointments, or frustrations don't get acknowledged, a major breakdown becomes all but inevitable. In the case of Drew and Shirley, this day had been years in the making. The problem wasn't just that Shirley didn't want to know how bad things were; Drew didn't want to say.

This combination of withholding and denial is a death sentence for many marriages. Coming out of denial can feel like having a bucket of ice water thrown in your face — not just once but repeatedly. The shock of revelation can be overwhelming, and often the initial impulse is to cut and run in order to stop the emotional pain that accompanies this revelation. And this is exactly what many couples do when faced with a painful reality.

Yet miraculously, in her moment of greatest pain, when Drew told Shirley their marriage was over, Shirley resisted the temptation to flee or retaliate. Caught between grief and rage, and facing a situation she had thought would never occur, she fought to contain her feelings. Drew was right about the marriage. It was over, at least in the form it had taken in recent years. The lies, withholding, and pretense were no longer part of their relationship. Yet the relationship itself, largely due to Shirley's commitment, did continue in a transformed state. Drew and Shirley stayed married, but they also created a marriage far more fulfilling than either had imagined could be possible.

This story is a cautionary tale about the consequences of making children and work a higher priority than the marriage. It reveals the power of intention, even when only one partner maintains his or her commitment, and provides some specific, practical steps a couple can take when they've hit the bottom of the pit of despair. Sometimes when we believe there's nothing more to lose, we find the strength and courage to recognize and fulfill our true dreams.

DREW: Shirley and I were high school sweethearts. We met when we were only sixteen. I knew from the very start that Shirley was the one — I had a strong sense early on that she was good for me. From the beginning, I was clear that I wanted to spend my life with her.

SHIRLEY: We dated throughout high school and college. As soon as we graduated from college, we got married. We were both just twenty-one.

DREW: I was happy and confident about our future. We had a lot of free time in those days, and we spent most of it together for the first three years. It was idyllic before the kids came, then things started to speed up. We were both working long hours, and we found ourselves spending less and less time together. In retrospect, I can see that we were way too busy. Over time our relationship began to deteriorate.

SHIRLEY: We were focused on the kids' best interests — they moved into the center of our lives, and our relationship took a back seat. We were also busy building our careers and our social life, working hard to manifest our goals. I was really enjoying the excitement of having a career. Having led a sheltered life while I was growing up, I was experiencing freedom for the first time.

From outward appearances, we were enjoying a happy, if not ideal, relationship. If I had been asked to give my marriage a rating, I would have said that, on a scale of zero to ten, it was a ten. That is, until the day Drew came home and dropped a bombshell. He walked in the door, asked me to sit down, and then said, "Our marriage is over." I couldn't believe my ears, so I asked him to repeat himself. "Our marriage is over," he said. "I can't live this way any more." He went on to tell me he'd been having an affair with one of my best friends for a little over a year.

It was probably the single worst moment of my life. I was overwhelmed with the strongest emotions I've ever felt: rage, pain, grief, confusion, and then more rage, more than I thought I was capable of feeling. I never believed until then that I was capable of killing anyone, but at that moment I knew I could.

No news is not necessarily good news

DREW: What for Shirley had been a ten was for me a zero. And it had been for a long time. I was considering leaving the marriage because I was miserable. Part of my distress derived from the fact that we had been preoccupied with kids and work for so long that we had lost all the intimacy in our relationship. We occasionally had sex, but we weren't making love. It was more like Shirley was performing her wifely duties. My disappointment and resentment grew by the day, but I kept it bottled up inside me.

I was too chicken and too proud to share my unhappiness with Shirley, so I acted it out instead. I never intended for the affair to go on for so long, but things just got out of hand. I kept putting off telling Shirley how dissatisfied I was with what felt like a dead marriage. It seemed like all the juice had gone out of it, and we were living like two roommates or siblings whose lives were consumed with work and domestic responsibilities. I was depressed and unhappy, and I blamed Shirley.

Admitting to the affair was one of the hardest things I've ever done. I knew Shirley would be furious and deeply hurt by my admission, and that's why I kept putting it off. I was hoping things would change — maybe it would all go away. I was in denial. And then I reached the point where I couldn't lie any more.

When I finally confronted Shirley and acknowledged the depth of my feelings of deprivation, I was shocked by her reaction. Rather than wanting to end our marriage, she stood up and fought to save it. The turning point came when we could each discuss our accountability for the affair. It didn't happen right away. We had to let out our feelings and hear each other out, which we did several times before we were finally able to look at our own parts in the breakdown. Both of us realized that we had been living a lie. We had been disconnected and had tried to cover it by acting like a happy family.

SHIRLEY: We had both been in serious denial. I had known that things weren't perfect between us, but I'd rationalized it all by telling myself that things weren't *that* bad. I was alone a lot, raising our kids mostly by myself, and I resented Drew pouring so much of himself into his career. As it turned out, we were both suffering in silence.

DREW: Instead of seeing herself as the injured party, Shirley began to take responsibility for her part in the breakdown. She had defined herself as a good wife by making a lovely home, cooking nutritious meals, working hard at her career, and being a loving mother. She realized that I had a very different definition of what constituted a good wife. She listened and made some changes. We started to enjoy each other again and remembered why we got together in the first place.

SHIRLEY: I knew Drew wasn't experiencing the love I felt for him because of the resentment I had layered over it. And I knew I had to do something about that besides express my anger. We both had to spend more time together and give some of what we were giving to our work and the kids to each other. I decided to show Drew that I loved him in ways he could experience.

We committed to three dates a week, times that we devoted exclusively to being with each other without interruptions by anyone, including the kids. We did some of the things we had done together during the early years, like going to bed early and feeding each other popcorn on weekends. I committed myself to deepening our sexual connection, which had been badly neglected. We made a joint decision to make our sexual contact a central part of our lives. I stopped sleeping in flannel pajamas, and together we went shopping for sexy lingerie. We bought some wonderful books and read to each other, which is something we both had always enjoyed. We read to each other in the bathtub, and we read to each other on the back-porch swing. We read books about love that catalyzed discussions about what love meant to us. We made time for each other for the first time in years, and held hands like we used to in high school.

Another important thing I did that helped us recover from the breakdown was resist the temptation to complain to my friends. At the beginning, I was strongly tempted to tell my side of the story and portray myself as the injured party — which is absolutely how I felt. I'm sure they would have taken my side, but then the recovery period would have been more difficult with the story out in the world. Instead I sought the support of an older woman friend I trusted to be discreet.

DREW: I grew up believing that the way you deal with bad feelings like sadness or pain is to stuff them or just get over them. "Boys don't cry," or hurt or get scared or have needs. Real men don't complain, they just suck it up — and that's exactly what I did, or at least tried to do. My desire to prove I was a man almost cost me my marriage. When I saw the pain I had created for Shirley, it cut me to the quick. I felt horrible. I didn't want her to suffer. Her pain awakened me from my numbness. I saw that she really did care about me; she was just busy and distracted. And I saw my own dishonesty in not letting her know how much I was suffering.

It was a time of huge changes for us. I began to tell the truth about what my needs were, and we both started being more honest with each other. Shirley's behavior changed so rapidly and so dramatically that I could no longer believe the story I had been telling myself — that she didn't really care about me, that she was taking me for granted. I couldn't continue denying her love even if I wanted to. Looking back on it, it's a miracle that we made it.

Forgiveness is a process, not an event

SHIRLEY: Not a miracle, but a result of our doing some damned hard work. But even with all the good work we did, which was considerable, it still took me three years to completely heal from the breakdown. Drew let me take the time I needed to heal and to repair the damaged trust. He never rushed me through the process or tried to get me to just let go and forgive. It meant a lot to me that Drew said, "Whenever you feel you don't trust me, tell me right away and I will address your concern, because I want you to trust me fully. You can tell me anything, anytime, anywhere. You can take as much time as you need to get through this."

DREW: I'm deeply grateful to Shirley for not quitting on our marriage like I thought she would when she found out about the affair.

SHIRLEY: Quit on the marriage? I was too angry to quit on it! It wasn't just that I wanted to salvage our twenty-year marriage, but I wasn't going to let you, or her, off the hook that easily!

DREW: Well, whatever your reason was, I'm glad we made it through that awful time, and I'm grateful for what we learned in the process.

SHIRLEY: It's the "C" word, *communication*. You've got to keep talking, even if it means you risk upsetting the applecart. In wanting to avoid an argument or some hurt feelings, we came within a razor's edge of losing our marriage. Another thing we learned is that it's okay to have upsets, in fact it's inevitable. You deal with them and get over them. But if you don't talk about things, problems don't go away. They go underground, and things just get worse. The way we learned how to handle disappointments and hard feelings was to get more experience dealing with them.

The most damaged trust can be repaired and strengthened

DREW: And we got plenty of practice! More than I wanted, but probably not more than we needed. With both of us coming from families where no one dealt openly with negative feelings, we needed to find out that differences don't kill you, and that not facing them may kill the marriage. I really did believe that day I admitted my affair that the marriage was over. I had already let go of the marriage when I came home and dropped the bomb on Shirley. I didn't think there was enough left to salvage, to even fight for. If Shirley hadn't taken a stand to save the marriage, we would have divorced.

Shirley and I had a lot of other opportunities to deal with differences and practice open communication after coming through this crisis in our marriage. We dealt more openly with not only our differences but also other family members and business associates. In our willingness to acknowledge our feelings and express them openly, we were able to neutralize smoldering problems before they became destructive crises.

We thought the worst was behind us — we had come so close to breaking up, and we were happy that we'd made it through the crisis.

SHIRLEY: When our daughter, Anne, entered high school, our neat, tidy, orderly family began to fall apart. Anne began to run around with a fast crowd, drinking and driving, and she got into several car accidents. Our model student started to bring home poor grades. We were alarmed and knew that something was wrong, but had no idea what it was. One day, the school counselors came to our home. They felt they needed to tell us that Anne had confided something very personal to them. She'd told a counselor that, several years earlier, she had been sexually molested by a relative.

DREW: When we confronted her, Anne denied the allegations. We found out months later that she had made a decision years earlier to never tell, because she didn't want to damage the family connections. It wasn't until Shirley, Anne, and I went into family counseling that the shadowy truth began to emerge. The incidents had taken place with a relative who babysat for us over a period of three years, when Anne was ten to thirteen. When we confronted the relative and family involved, all hell broke loose. The extended family refused therapy, and the relative would not go to the sex offenders program. We were devastated.

SHIRLEY: I cried every day for six months, but we stayed in counseling, and over time, Anne made significant headway. She expressed her confusion, hurt, and pain, and made a good recovery. But the rift with my in-laws was severe. Their refusal to address the issues responsibly resulted in my not speaking to them for years.

DREW: It was many years before we fully repaired the damage caused by that breach of trust, that violation, but we did finally recover. We got good help, which made a huge difference. What I learned most was to stand by my woman! It wasn't about agreeing with whatever she said; it was about respecting what she said and felt and believed, and being fully supportive.

SHIRLEY: Drew's support helped me to trust myself more, and over time I became able to make contact with the molester's family again. At first I could bear being with them for only twenty or thirty minutes at a time, but eventually I began to see them differently and realized they weren't fundamentally mean people; they were just overwhelmed themselves and had no idea how to deal with the situation. Now it's much easier to be in their presence. The big lesson for me has been forgiveness.

DREW: Life is really good now. I never imagined that being with a partner could ever be this rich. When I need her the most, Shirley comes through. I'm so glad we were both willing to do the work that enabled us to experience how sweet it is now.

SHIRLEY: Drew is a genuinely generous person and an incredible mentor. He believes in me, and he always supports me in whatever I'm doing. He's never said to me, "You can't do that." There's rarely a day that I don't let him know one way or another how appreciative I am.

DREW: It's hard to believe we not only survived those crises but also came through them stronger and more loving than before. We're basically simple, ordinary folks. If we can do it, anyone can!

8.

FAILURE IS AN ESSENTIAL STEP ON THE ROAD TO SUCCESS

Liza and Raz Ingrasci

Sometimes difficulties can feel overwhelming, and then no amount of hopeful thinking can provide relief. These are the times when the benefits of a strong relationship really come into play. But not all couples create a secure and trustworthy foundation that sustains them throughout a crisis. Like many others in this book, Raz and Liza have had their share of life's challenges, even though others around them have always viewed theirs as an ideal life. What was not apparent even to many of their friends was the series of ordeals they faced, and ultimately grew in response to, throughout their thirty-year marriage. Raz and Liza didn't try to conceal their challenges from others. Rather, they met them with the same acceptance, mutual support, and commitment that they brought to all aspects of their lives.

When Raz was at his lowest points in life and unable to find the strength and confidence to go forward, he was able to borrow Liza's conviction and confidence in him. We can all use the reassurance and perspectives of those who really know us, those who can see us clearly when our own perceptions are distorted by self-recrimination or negativity. In times when we are consumed with self-doubt, guilt, shame, or feelings of inadequacy, a trusted loved one's ability to reflect our own goodness back to us can make the difference between our giving up and breaking through. Raz came through his ordeal stronger than before. Later he had the opportunity to reciprocate the gift Liza had given him by supporting her as their family went through yet another crisis, one that ultimately deepened their love even further.

Cycles of reciprocal giving and receiving characterize all great relationships. Partners in such relationships deeply believe that, in the process of mutual caregiving and support, no one needs to keep score. This trust is grounded in the knowledge that the rewards of giving are immediate, sustaining, and inherent in the process. Inevitably, an environment of abundant generosity and goodwill influences the lives of others. We are changed by what we experience in, and give to, the relationship. What we give to others and how we engage them is also changed. People in fulfilling, loving relationships are kinder to, more considerate of, and more respectful to others simply because they have more to give. The relationship itself becomes the wellspring from which the waters of generosity flow.

RAZ: Liza and I were working for the same organization when we met. The first time she walked into the room where we were having a meeting, I saw light all around her, literally. It was a magic moment.

LIZA: I was a little bit slower than Raz, but it didn't take me long to see that Raz was a man with wisdom and vision.

RAZ: We were very happy during our early years together, but there was one sticking place that gave us trouble. I've always been a good communicator, especially in the workplace. Maybe it comes from my love of and fascination with language and the power of words. But the same skills that enabled me to be effective on the job often got me into trouble at home.

Not winning doesn't necessarily mean losing

RAZ: I've probably learned more about communication from my marriage with Liza than I've learned from all of my jobs and formal education put together. Those lessons have been powerful, but at times also painful. One of my strengths is that I'm generally able to remain cool and collected in conversations, even when they get heated. I've always been able to control my emotions so that they don't get in the way of my rational thinking, and I can usually reason my way through situations.

I learned, though, that there are times when it isn't necessary or even desirable to win an argument, and that *not* winning doesn't necessarily mean losing. During the first few years of our marriage, I used my debating skills to try to outwit Liza whenever we got into an argument. Since we're both strong-willed people, this was not an infrequent occurrence! Liza is much more emotional than I am. Unlike me, she doesn't tend to live in her head. She is connected to her feelings, and she expresses them spontaneously and freely. I have always been more deliberate and guarded in what I say and, therefore, tend to be more logical and rational in conversations. Early on when Liza and I would get into arguments, we would both raise our voices and interrupt the other, but I could almost always outargue her and remain cool and collected while calmly pointing out how illogical and unreasonable she was being. The more logical I got, the more emotional Liza would become, until eventually she would get hysterical. These disputes would end with Liza in tears feeling defeated, leaving me with a hollow victory because she was so lifeless in her defeat. The negative energy between us could remain for days.

Vulnerability isn't a weakness; it's a strength

RAZ: When our daughter, Marissa, was six years old, I began to notice that I had a very different way of being with her when she was hurt or upset. I was always sweet and patient with her. When Marissa was hurting, I wouldn't talk much to her at all. I would just hold her in my arms and try to comfort her until she quieted down and felt better. Then she would get up as if nothing had happened and return to whatever she had been doing prior to her upset. It dawned on me one day that there was a vulnerable little six-year-old inside of Liza who didn't need to be argued with or convinced of anything. She just needed to be loved. I realized that being a champion debater was a dubious honor in marriage. It certainly wasn't bringing me closer to my wife. It was at this point that I learned to be emotionally flexible with Liza.

I was committed to bringing this insight into our marriage, and discovered that, with my newly found determination to be a more loving husband, I was able to gradually overcome my decades-long pattern of verbal manipulation. I don't need to win arguments and defeat Liza anymore, and I don't want to. We both lose when I do that. Nowadays, when I become aware that I have done or said things that hurt or disturb her, I just tell her, "I'm sorry I hurt your feelings."

LIZA: Our love for each other is very strong, and that was powerful motivation to find a way to deal with this ghastly pattern. I realized that when I simply told Raz I felt lost, it would cue him to slow down and observe what he was doing. I tried a lot of things to change the pattern. I tried winking at him; sometimes I kicked him under the table. The bottom line is that we were both committed to getting past this cycle. It's just excruciatingly painful when we're disconnected. One of the things that helped us most was our willingness to sit down after a stressful interaction and really look at our behavior. The question we addressed was "What happened?"

RAZ: After working as an executive for several years, I decided to start my own business. Although Liza and I were both aware of the risks, we were confident that I would be as successful on my own as I had been as a corporate employee. The reality of a start-up, however, turned out to be quite different from the scenario either of us had imagined.

Three years into my venture, I found myself in a tough position. I had lost all my initial capital through a series of misjudgments and magical thinking. Making matters infinitely worse was the fact that, through what I believed to be rock-solid tax planning with a reputable firm, I had failed to pay sufficient tax. It wasn't until four years later that I became aware of the shortfall, and by that time, with all the penalties and interest factored in, my tax debt came to more than $150,000! When the IRS contacted me with the news, I went into shock. This had to be a mistake. But it wasn't, and they meant business. We worked out a payment plan that allowed me to pay off the debt over time at a low interest rate, but I still had to pay it all. It was like being knocked down and kicked in the gut.

Lessons in humility may cause us to eat our words, which can be very nourishing

RAZ: I felt humiliated and devastated by this massive financial crisis. In addition to feeling ashamed of myself for this failure, I was deeply concerned for the well-being of my family. Not only was our income insufficient to pay the bills mounting up, but there were no apparent prospects that could alter what appeared to be certain and imminent disaster. I'd felt confident and optimistic going into the business, and now, four years later, we were broke and I was broken. I felt worthless.

LIZA: While I knew we were in real trouble financially, I didn't see the situation as hopeless or terminal. I also didn't see it as being all Raz's fault and didn't hold him entirely responsible for the way things had turned out. Raz didn't make these decisions unilaterally; I'd provided input into everything. Had there been something I didn't believe in that he wanted to do, I would have objected. Yes, there were things I had my doubts about, and looking back, maybe I should have taken a stronger stand. That's my part in things. But I trusted Raz, and in general I trust his judgment. We've always operated as a team, and I think my more conservative views provide a good balance for his tendency toward risk-taking and boldness. On this one, we missed the boat — not just Raz, both of us.

RAZ: Liza never used the crisis as a means of shaming me. Her response was the opposite.

LIZA: To me, this wasn't a failure; it was just a financial setback with some major lessons for both of us. He was being too hard on himself. I just wanted him to forgive himself and trust that we would dig our way out of this hole together.

RAZ: I didn't feel worthy of Liza's forgiveness, and couldn't forgive myself, but she was relentless. She kept reassuring me that things were going to work out, and that she loved me as much as ever.

LIZA: Unbeknown to Raz at the time, I was conspiring with several other people to surprise him with a fortieth birthday party. I invited several dozen people from his life, past and present — including old schoolmates, friends from previous jobs, and family members he hadn't seen in years. Friends and family flew in from all over the country.

RAZ: No one breathed a word, and I never suspected a thing. When I walked into that room and saw all those faces, I was shocked, overwhelmed. It was just too much. I really felt their love, and I saw how happy they all were to be there, with me. It's a good thing I hadn't known what was going on, because if I had I never would have allowed the party to take place. I felt so utterly unworthy at that time. It was right in the middle of our financial meltdown, and I would never have been able to face all those people. But thanks to Liza's masterful scheming ability, I didn't have a chance to back out. It was an unbelievable night. I'll never forget it.

LIZA: The party was a turning point in our lives. It seemed that from then on, Raz began feeling better about himself. His energy and enthusiasm started coming back, and he started trusting me more. We stopped focusing on the mistakes of the past and started talking realistically about taking practical steps in our future. A short time later, Raz was offered a good job with a great salary. It would mean the end, at least for the time being, of our dream of building a company of our own, but we both realized that we couldn't say no to this opportunity. It was like a gift from heaven. Raz accepted the position. With his earnings we were able to pay off our debts and even put some income aside.

RAZ: There were blessings in that disastrous experience that I couldn't have predicted or even imagined. I hadn't realized how much I had linked my self-worth to money. In retrospect, I see that I really did believe my value as a human being was a function of my wealth. That whole experience, and Liza's unwavering support for me throughout it, shattered that belief. I finally got that she loved me not for my ability to bring in money but for myself, for the decent human being I am. That lesson is worth more than all the money in the world!

Then a few years after our recovery from financial disaster, we were challenged again. Because we were both working full-time to provide for the material needs of our family, we had needed a caregiver for the children. And so we had hired Mattie.

LIZA: Mattie wasn't just any nanny or au pair. She was a deeply loving, caring woman whom I trusted unconditionally to take care of our children. My trust in Mattie wasn't blind and wasn't based on belief or hope. She had been my own nanny when I was a child growing up in New York.

When Marissa was six months old, we had contacted Mattie and asked if she'd be willing to relocate to California to work for us as a live-in nanny. Although Mattie planned to retire to North Carolina, she had accepted the offer and, within a few weeks, had moved across the country and into our home and was essentially managing the household. We immediately became dependent on her. She was truly a part of our family.

RAZ: After Mattie had been living and working with us for five years, she was misdiagnosed as having a hernia, which later was determined to be advanced cancer. Suddenly our lives were in complete upheaval.

LIZA: Mattie, who had been taking care of everything, was now the one in need of care. Not only could she no longer do her job, she needed twenty-four-hour-a-day support. We knew there was no way we could do anything other than keep Mattie at home, provide her with the care that she needed, and give back some of the love and devotion she had given to us over the years.

RAZ: Mattie's transition from caregiver to care-receiver challenged us in ways that we didn't anticipate. She was an active member of her church community, and she had hundreds of devoted friends who adored her. When news of her illness spread through the community, our home almost immediately became the gathering place for her friends, who were constantly visiting her with gifts, meals, and beautiful energy. Lots of it!

LIZA: Mattie was one remarkably gregarious person who had spent much of her free time giving of herself to her ever-expanding network of friends. She was a people-magnet whose love and generosity drew many into her life. While dying she was continually buoyed up by the spirit of her friends, who were around her twenty-four hours a day.

During that time our family became closer and more openhearted than ever. Mattie's dying itself was a gift to the family. It not only opened our hearts but also provoked conversations within the family, conversations that helped us all to deepen and redefine our spiritual understanding in ways we had never done before. We spoke with the kids about our beliefs about life and death and the hereafter, and about what we saw as the purpose of our lives.

"There are no great acts, only small acts done with great love." — Mother Teresa

LIZA: I'd always known that Raz was a kind and generous man, but I had never witnessed it to the degree that I did during the final months of Mattie's life. I didn't expect him to be as willing to give back to her as I was. After all it was me, not him, who had a history with Mattie since childhood. I was deeply moved by his devotion to her, and witnessing it greatly deepened my love and respect for him. This was the time in my life when I learned to live with an open heart. No, it's the time that I learned to live with a broken heart.

If I had any advice for young couples, it would be to embrace the challenges instead of pushing them away. What has held us steady has been our assumption that, no matter what is going on, there are powerful lessons to be learned. The more stressful the life circumstances, the bigger the opportunity for some big lessons. It's a shame to push such opportunities away. Lean into the challenge; be willing to face it, whatever it is.

We've both learned to trust that, when we look at our life circumstances honestly, without being attached to any particular outcome, things work out. I have had to learn to lightly hold on to how I want things to turn out. As I learned to let go of preconceptions about how things should be, Raz and I became more cooperative in a creative way. Together we manifest things that are much greater than either of us could possibly create alone.

RAZ: Sooner or later most couples are challenged in unwanted ways that they never imagined. We certainly were. Your heart breaks, and you feel great pain. But the good news is that, when your heart breaks open, you can love more fully and more deeply than ever before. It's a chance to finally learn to live with an open heart.

9.

PLAY IS SERIOUS BUSINESS

Rich and Antra Borofsky

Antra and Rich Borofsky are psychologists and relationship therapists. But unlike many counselors, whose knowledge comes from classrooms and academic textbooks, theirs is grounded in the college of the real world. Many of their most important teachings originated in their own lives and, as a result, have the authenticity that comes only from direct experience. They demand as much, if not more, from themselves and each other as they do from their clients and the students who attend their workshops. One striking thing about the two of them is that they do it all with a light touch. Balancing humor and play with honesty and vulnerability is, for many couples, a supreme challenge, but as we discovered in our conversation with them, Rich and Antra do so with grace and ease.

Life for this couple is much more than a series of challenges, expectations, and requirements, however; it is an ongoing dance. This is not simply a metaphor: through dance and play and fearlessly honest self-expression, Rich and Antra provide examples of how two people can each day take delight in their own lives, their relationship, and their interactions with others.

Inevitably, however, they did find bumps along the way. The secret, according to Rich and Antra, is to meet those bumps with a shared intention to learn from them and use the difficulties to build personal integrity and create deeper trust, respect, and passion in the relationship. This is not simply a good idea or a theory for them but an ongoing practice that improves with age. One of the many things we learned from them is that the ability to play together is as important as the ability to work out differences. The more fun that couples enjoy together, the less the differences matter — in fact, they tend to appreciate the differences more. Rich and Antra have deepened each other's capacities for fun, creativity, and passion far beyond what most couples ever experience.

ANTRA: From the beginning, we knew we were a good match. On our first date, we went to an art museum. We found a large room full of paintings depicting the Pieta (Mary holding the body of her dead son, Jesus). I took one look around and whispered to Rich, "Let's be the paintings." Without hesitation, he laid himself across my lap and went completely limp — just like the body of Jesus in one of the paintings, his arms and head hanging down on one side of me, his legs hanging to the floor on the other. I mirrored the compassionate, beatific pose of Mary in the painting. After a few minutes in this pose, we moved to the next painting and then the next, each time taking turns being Mary and Jesus. Occasionally, other museumgoers would wander by as if nothing unusual were going on. After a half hour of enacting the paintings, I thought to myself, "This is the guy for me!"

Both of us are passionate people; passion is an enormously important aspect of our relationship. I'm talking not only about a passion for pleasurable experiences but also about a passion for the full depth and range of experiences that life has to offer. Of course, we enjoy all the positive experiences we have had, but we also make room for the painful parts of life. We've learned that, unless we can step into the difficult and painful experiences that unavoidably come up, our capacity to love is limited. We try to use everything in our relationship to deepen and enrich our loving.

> "A relationship is like a shark;
> it has to keep moving or it will die." — Woody Allen

RICH: One way to describe our relationship is as a continuous dance. We are always dancing — in the kitchen, in our work together, in the supermarket, during an argument, driving in the car, in bed. Everything we do is a dance. Sometimes it is the angry dance of self-righteous enemies; sometimes it's the tired dance of aging, aching complainers; and sometimes it's the close, slow dancing of lovers and best friends.

ANTRA: There's also a lot of stillness in our being together. We often listen to music. We spend a lot of time just enjoying the beauty of sitting silently together.

RICH: And we love ballroom dancing. But when we first started dancing, we had intense struggles over who was leading and who was following, who knew the right steps or moves, and so on. Some of our worst fights occurred on the dance floor in public. It was very embarrassing for me.

ANTRA: One of my most favorite ways of dancing together is ice dancing. Rich used to be a hockey player, and he's a really good ice skater. Many years ago, I decided to take up skating. I took lessons for years, lots and lots of lessons, and eventually became a pretty good skater. Then I talked him into giving up his hockey skates for figure skates, which was not easy for a hockey player to do. Now we do ice dancing together. I love the way we move and flow together while gliding across the ice. It feels completely natural and effortless. Often it's not clear which of us is leading and which is following. At these moments I feel we are dissolving into each other and into oneness. For me, skating together to music we both love, looking into each other's eyes, is heaven on ice.

RICH: Another thing we have learned to do is to play with our differences so that they make us more alive rather than cause conflict.

ANTRA: When our differences arise, we usually let them collide, but with more awareness. You could say we've learned how to have controlled collisions. We no longer take our collisions so personally or seriously. It's like driving the bumper cars in amusement parks.

Most of the time, we don't work on our issues so much as play with them. For example, both of us are very competitive, and instead of seeing it as a problem or trying to conceal or stop our competitiveness, we do the opposite: we make it explicit. So we might have an open competition and keep score. Once we got into an absurd competition to determine which of us was the most loving.

RICH: My favorite competition was the one to determine which of us was the least competitive. I also really liked the competition, which we still sometimes have, called the "Victim Olympics." This is a competition to see who is the bigger victim. Each of us gets equal time to complain about how hard and unfair our life is. We each then get a score on how well we have portrayed ourselves as victims.

ANTRA: We are both constantly learning from whatever happens between us. When we do or say something that doesn't work, we try to understand why. I might ask Rich, "What part of what I just offered you could you take in, and what part couldn't you?" It's often the tone, rather than the content, that's the problem.

If at first you don't succeed...

RICH: Often Antra will say, "I don't have a problem with what you're saying to me, but I do with the way you're saying it."

ANTRA: Then I'll say, "Are you willing to try again?" We do a second take. For a while we even used a clapboard — you know, one of those things that they use in movies when they're repeating a scene. We would clap the top down and yell, "Take two," then begin the dialogue again. Sometimes we'd take nine or ten takes to get it right. Getting it right means that we are trying to make contact with each other in a way that is authentic, respectful, trusting, lively, and kind.

RICH: We are willing to do this because we see our relationship as a practice. It's not something that happens spontaneously. We are willing to practice because that's the only way to improve the quality of our communication and our connection.

ANTRA: My feelings of greatest vulnerability come up when I get criticized. Before we became conscious of our hot buttons, or sore spots, we caused each other a great deal of pain. We had a lot of fights and misunderstandings. But once I became aware of Rich's sensitivity to feeling controlled, I could address the issue at its core. I would say to him, "You're free." Just saying those two words worked like a charm. It was amazing. Of course, I had to learn to let go of my own need to control him when I felt anxious, or when I had a strong preference, in order to say this genuinely.

RICH: The magic words we discovered that helped Antra when she got defensive were: "I love you just the way you are." This stopped any argument in its tracks. Discovering the antidote to our greatest fears and vulnerabilities has saved us a great deal of heartache. Awareness is the most important element of our relationship. Without it our relationship would be hell. We would repeat the same negative patterns of interaction over and over and never learn anything. That's my definition of hell.

ANTRA: My practice is to become better able to say "yes" to everything that our life together presents: difficulty or ease, pleasure or pain, anger or delight, desire or aversion, love or hatred. To accept it, to feel all this and not act it out, is my everyday practice. It may seem paradoxical, but I keep discovering that the more I accept the negative, the more the positive shows up in all kinds of ways.

RICH: I'd say the second-most important element of our relationship is that we are always learning. The main thing we're interested in learning is what love is and how it actually works. What we've learned has enabled us to keep renewing and growing our love.

ANTRA: And when you distill love down to its essence, it is simply attention. Our love is renewed by consciously and skillfully giving and receiving attention.

We discovered this model when we first got together and Rich was working on his doctoral thesis. One evening, he was seated at his desk, deeply absorbed in writing, when I came over and asked in an anxious tone, "Do you love me?"

RICH: Antra's question annoyed me. I felt interrupted, and I didn't understand what she wanted from me. I was not able to switch from what I was doing to tell her genuinely that I loved her. I felt put on the spot. However, fortunately I was sufficiently aware to see that her question "Do you love me?" was actually a request for some loving attention.

ANTRA: He asked me, "Are you needing some love right now?" I thought about this for a moment and then, with some embarrassment and awkwardness, answered, "Yes, I'm needing some love right now."

RICH: So I asked her another question: "Are you ready to receive some love right now?" She looked inside herself and saw she was experiencing a lot of anxiety, and that she actually wasn't ready to take anything in. She said, "To tell you the truth, I'm not ready to receive your love." So I asked her, "Could you make yourself ready?"

ANTRA: I took a few moments, closed my eyes, took a deep breath, and opened up a space of greater receptivity inside myself. Then I heard Rich gently asking me to open my eyes when I was ready. When I opened them, we were both open and available to each other.

RICH: The way Antra looked at me when she opened her eyes was irresistible.

ANTRA: With his whole heart, Rich said, "I love you." I was able to fully take it in and let myself be fed by his love. It was completely nourishing. We have come to understand that the quality of the attention we give and receive is what determines the level of fulfillment and connection and love that we experience with each other.

RICH: In this example you can see that being aware of *how* we give and receive can make a huge difference. For an exchange to work, the receiver has to consciously offer his or her need, make a space to receive what is needed, welcome fully what is actually available in the present, and feel the gratitude that appears when one receives deeply. This way of consciously receiving inspires the giver to gather, offer, aim, and release to the other the fullness of whatever he or she has to give. When we are conscious of how we give and receive, then everything that is shared, no matter whether it is positive or negative, feels like a great gift.

ANTRA: We can work our way out of anything because we have faith that everything is workable, and that whatever happens is all grist for the mill. In our work, we're trying to help couples see how they can offer their pain and anger to each other in a way that lets them connect, rather than disconnect.

RICH: What makes our faith so strong is that we've learned how love actually works. It's fairly simple. Love is simply the art of attentiveness. In our relationship we are constantly trying to refine the quality of our attention to every exchange or interaction. In this sense, we're really artists in the way we approach communication. We're always trying to find the most authentic and effective ways of connecting.

ANTRA: We're both trying to better receive each other's feedback about how we speak and listen to each other. For example, if I offer Rich an apology, I may think that what I'm offering is heartfelt.

RICH: But from my perspective it might look like a C+ apology. So we'll talk about it, and maybe I'll say something like "Could you give me your A apology?" And because she was already doing her best, she might say, "Can you show me what an A apology would look like to you?" I'll then try to offer her my very best apology.

ANTRA: Rich's willingness to show me his best apology allows me to try again, to be more vulnerable or more humble in my next message. One of the powerful things in our relationship is that we've always been experimenters. Whenever we get a new idea from anywhere, we immediately start to play with it. There's a tremendous amount of creativity, freedom, and flexibility in that.

You must be present to win

ANTRA: One of the gifts Rich has brought to me, primarily through his practice, is his ability to stay present even when strong emotions arise.

He's challenged me many times to not run away from what's painful, and that's been a gift because it has helped me develop my capacity to be with pain rather than passing it on to others. When I try to get rid of my pain, it inevitably ends up getting directed at someone else in the form of blame or anger. Whenever I can stay with it, I usually learn something important.

When I was young, I loved the feeling of falling in love. I was addicted to the intensity of this feeling of falling in love. Now my loving is big enough to include not loving. It includes everything, so it has no opposite. That's the way we see relationship. It has to include everything, because every relationship is a microcosm of the whole human condition.

RICH: Sex has always been an important part of our relationship. Like every other part of our relationship, it has improved greatly as a result of our being present and paying close attention to how we give ourselves and receive each other sexually.

ANTRA: Rich's willingness to learn how to be receptive sexually has made a huge difference for me. I remember many years ago feeling so tired at the end of the day. We would get into bed and Rich would reach for me, and I would immediately become anxious thinking that he wanted to make love. All I could feel in response, was a strong "No, I'm too tired; leave me alone!"

RICH: Antra's negative response would stir up my feelings of hurt and rejection. Eventually, I became curious about why this was not working. I discovered to my surprise that, when I shifted into being completely receptive, with no attachment to what might happen, she became more interested in sex.

ANTRA: Now when Rich comes to bed, he'll often lie down next to me, completely relaxed. We just enjoy the pleasure and warmth of being near each other. His being so receptive will often spark my sexual interest. I can intuit that he's thinking about sex, and then my thoughts start to flow in that pattern too. Before long, one of us moves a leg a bit closer, and our body heat starts to rise. I often move slowly from my tired "no" to a "maybe" to an enthusiastic "yes!"

RICH: By being deeply receptive, I find that sex now feels more like a gift we receive with gratitude than a need that has to be gratified.

ANTRA: And instead of seeing Rich as trying to get or take something from me, I now see him as offering me something of great beauty.

RICH: But of course, this is true not just of sex. It's become clear to us, after thirty-eight years together, that everything we do with each other is a form of lovemaking. There are a million ways to say "I love you."

10.

HUMBLE BEGINNINGS CAN BE THE SOURCE OF GREAT ACHIEVEMENTS

Barbara and Larry Dossey

Larry and Barbara didn't begin their careers in medicine with a desire to become world-renowned experts in alternative forms of healing. Their efforts to heal some of their own personal health issues forced them to go beyond the limits of conventional medicine in their beliefs, practices, and teaching. Although they encountered a number of challenging circumstances professionally and personally, marital difficulty was not one of them. They used the ever-growing strength of their relationship to create a base from which to meet the skepticism, doubt, and judgmental attitude with which conventional medical professionals initially greeted their work.

Since they began their work together in 1968, Larry and Barbara have accomplished far more than they ever anticipated they could. Larry has written ten books, several of them bestsellers, and Barbara has authored or coauthored twenty. They have also written or contributed to dozens of articles about the mind-body connection. Views that were seen as recently as twenty years ago as unscientific, unconventional, even irresponsible have largely, as a result of the Dosseys' pioneering efforts, become integrated into accepted mainstream medical knowledge and practice.

According to both Larry and Barbara, their accomplishments are primarily a result of relationships in their personal and professional lives. Perhaps one of their greatest achievements has been to create and maintain supportive connections with each other, colleagues, and friends throughout the world. Both are certain that they could never have achieved what they have without those alliances. Their story reflects the power of supportive relationships, and it provides examples of how to create high-powered connections with others, connections that can create a bridge between a dream and reality.

LARRY: I came from humble beginnings. I was born on a farm, two and a half months premature, in a poor area of Texas. My grandparents came in and took over, making an incubator out of two dresser drawers propped up by the fireplace for my twin brother and me. Later, when I became a doctor, I calculated the chances of both twins surviving under such conditions to be one in a hundred.

No one in the history of my family had ever gone beyond the tenth grade — they had all been farmers. My parents were sharecroppers; they didn't even own the land they worked. My brother and I started a new tradition of achievement and education, and my family sacrificed everything they had to help us get ahead, which is a debt I can never repay. I never felt deprived, although we were as poor as church mice. We had no running water and no electricity. I believe that as long as kids have love, they don't care if they live in a palace or a hut. I come from a line of hardy, hardworking people; I never take anything for granted, and I live in gratitude for the breaks that come my way.

Our wounds can call forth our greatest gifts

BARBARA: We both had passionate calls to service. It was in my second year of nursing school that I fell in love with nursing. As a young nurse, I worked on a critical care unit with many critically ill patients. I just loved the combination of high tech and high touch. In my early years I loved taking care of patients when I could hear their stories.

I had a severe eye infection that left me with compromised vision in one eye, after an extremely painful recovery. Going through that critical eye crisis and postcorneal transplant, I practiced self-healing, utilizing meditation, breath work, and music that could control the potential of corneal rejection. These alternative treatments really helped me, and I couldn't wait to pass on what I was learning to others. Had I not had that experience, the focus of my work would have been very different. This was the beginning of my own transpersonal orientation to medicine, born of my own wound. Larry's practice of holistic healing and transpersonal medicine also was influenced by painful personal experience.

LARRY: Since I was a child, I've suffered with migraine headaches. Worse than the pain, nausea, and vomiting with a migraine was the temporary blindness. The headaches made it impossible for me to focus on anything, and they came very close to ending my medical career even before it got started. When I was still in medical school, I realized that even temporary blindness during a migraine could cause me to inadvertently harm or even kill someone. I was horrified by that possibility. For ethical reasons, I decided to quit school even though being a doctor was what I wanted more than anything. It was a painful decision, but I didn't see any other option. When I consulted my advisor about leaving, he talked me out of it, insisting that eventually the intractable headaches would go away. He was wrong; they didn't. In fact they got worse.

I had tried all the traditional medical treatments, and nothing worked. This was in the early days of biofeedback, and for most doctors that was still a dirty word. It was something that kooks and flakes practiced. But I knew enough about it to know that biofeedback had real healing potential. In desperation, I went outside the traditional medical treatments, chasing all over the country to learn biofeedback. In those days the equipment was not easy to obtain. I had to purchase biofeedback machinery from Holland.

I set up the equipment in my office, and after I learned to use it on myself to treat my migraines, I began teaching the process to my patients and others. Then one day some U.S. customs agents came into my office, flashed their badges, and confiscated all my equipment. They just took it all away, no explanation, no receipt, nothing. I never heard from them again. By then it was possible to purchase American-made equipment to replace the confiscated machines, and soon I was back in business.

BARBARA: Larry and I were working in a large traditional hospital setting in Texas in the early seventies. He had a busy medical practice. We invited a group of about thirty professionals, including psychologists, nurses, doctors, and allied health professionals to meet with us on a monthly basis. We all had an interest in cutting-edge medical treatments and alternative healing methods. In our meetings, we would enter into dialogue about various modalities that we were using with our patients and what results we were getting. Sometimes we would invite guest presenters. One time we had a Hispanic shaman come and demonstrate how he would take an illness out of a person. We were open to anything.

LARRY: Our relationship has consisted, in part, of taking on book projects focused on nonconformist topics. Many of the things we wrote articles about thirty years ago are currently accepted in the culture. But when we first began, we got a lot of criticism. The fact that both Barbie and I have been outstanding medical professionals has made us bulletproof. We have been on the cutting edge, exploring unconventional treatments.

BARBARA: We haven't had to go through rough patches or separations in our marriage. The fireworks were only those coming at us, not between us. These actually made us and our connection stronger.

Your support network
does not have to be limited by geography

LARRY: We both have a great capacity to reach out. We have a huge network with a broad base of support, and we have been blessed with a global community, where we share ideas and come up with new ways to build partnerships. With our worldwide network, we explore our mutual interests and often become collaborators in incredibly fascinating projects.

Of all the challenges I have experienced in my life, the greatest, and the one in which Barbie's support was most meaningful, had nothing to do with my work but was much more personal. Several years ago, we had been traveling and were spending the night in a hotel. It was too early to go to bed, and I was mindlessly flipping through the channels on TV, channel surfing, trying to find something interesting to watch. I stopped at a made-for-TV movie about Vietnam that featured a bunch of young soldiers. They were just kids. The movie was an embodiment of my worst nightmare, a recurring dream that I had experienced dozens of times since my days in Vietnam.

I had enlisted in the army and gone to Vietnam as a battalion surgeon, which means I spent most of my time carrying an aid bag and a rifle and being shot at in the field. When I went into the service, I promised my parents I would never take unnecessary risks. Within weeks I had renounced that vow and had volunteered for a lot of high-risk assignments. I did manage to survive, but I owe a large part of my survival to dumb luck. Part of the price I paid was more than twenty years of horrible nightmares. I never discussed my experiences in the war with anyone, not even Barbie.

A caring presence can be the best support

LARRY: For some reason when I came to this movie about Vietnam, I didn't skip over it like I normally would have. I felt compelled to watch it. The movie was identical to my recurring nightmare. A bunch of young soldiers, no more than kids, were separated from their weapons, and the Vietcong were closing in. The soldiers were helpless and terrified. They knew they were going to die. I watched the whole movie, and when it ended I began crying. Not just weeping, but deep gut-wrenching sobs that shook my whole body. I couldn't stop. I cried nearly the whole night long. I'd never experienced anything like it. But it was Barb who made it possible for me to get through it. I couldn't have made it without her. She hung in there with me through every moment of my experience.

BARBARA: I really didn't do anything, and I mean that literally. I just sat with him to bear witness to his suffering and pain. I didn't say anything. I knew Larry was going through something terribly important and that, although he was obviously in great pain, he was also perfectly okay. I just sat there with him for hours, listening and being with him. My being there with my heart open seemed to help him to be with and bear his pain.

Many hours later, Larry stopped crying and said he needed to go for a walk alone. When he finally came back, there was another layer of pain for him to experience. I just held the space for him to be with his pain, remaining as fully present with him as I could possibly be, so that he could stay with his experience and go right down to the bottom of it, as far as possible.

LARRY: After that night of catharsis, the nightmares went away and never came back. Going through this episode of terrible anguish has deepened our capacity to be present with suffering.

BARBARA: Just like everything else we have learned personally about healing, it immediately went into the work we do with others. We have come to call this work "sacred service." The process of working with intense pain is to make a place for it, and to keep breathing into it to allow the pain to show itself. In that process, both people strive to come to a deeper understanding and acceptance by bearing witness.

Vacations can be the most productive times of your life

BARBARA: Every summer, we spend six weeks by the high mountain lakes of Wyoming and Montana. We ride in on horseback and camp at an elevation of twelve thousand feet. Anything can happen — snow, wind, rain, and bears. We really connect, and we bond very closely. It's always an amazing experience. We use the time away from the world of responsibility to do our own deep personal work. We challenge each other and ourselves by asking penetrating questions such as "What am I doing my work for? Is my ego involved in any way? Am

I taking good care of myself while I serve? Am I doing my work with integrity? Am I being ruthlessly honest with myself about my real reasons for doing this work?"

LARRY: We each take at least one trip alone every season to balance out our heavy consulting schedule, but the trip into the mountains is always the biggest trip of the year. When we're on it, we always do a life assessment and look deeply into our purpose and see how we're doing. I can't imagine accomplishing the work output that we pull off without the assessment and strategic planning we do when we go up into the mountains. We always get deeply renewed being in the midst of the majesty of nature for so many weeks. And it is the exquisite nature of our relationship that enables us to do our cutting-edge work.

BARBARA: We both have a strong work ethic. We work hard and write all day long. At the end of the day, we take a long walk, create an easy, nutritious meal, and both do needlepoint. We often work on each other's pieces. Needlepoint is a form of weaving and a metaphor for our lives, since we literally weave our lives and our work together in one big colorful tapestry. We actually put a piece of each other's hair in our weaving. It's symbolic of putting ourselves, bodily, into what we do. The blending of our ideas and energies is the creative process of our lives together. We're not trying to change the world, just to embody our passion and healing in a way that will make the world a better place.

11.

LOVE CREATES MIRACLES

Mariah and Ron Gladis

The first thing we noticed about Mariah was her eyes. Brilliant, piercing, and penetrating, they were sparkling with aliveness. We were immediately drawn into her world, and we both felt she could see deeply into ours. It was a sense of connection that was almost frightening.

The second thing we noticed about her was equally striking, though in a different way: the quality of her speech. Her words clearly did not emanate from a strong, healthy body. As we strained to comprehend, her husband, Ron, interpreted for her, as he would for the remainder of the interview. Rail thin, Mariah inhabits a body that has been wracked by the ravages of ALS (amyotrophic lateral sclerosis), or Lou Gehrig's disease. The survival expectancy for people with ALS is less than five years on average. Mariah was diagnosed with the disease more than twenty-eight years ago, and she has not simply beaten the odds, she's destroyed them. It would not be an overstatement to call her a living miracle.

But Ron and Mariah's story is much bigger than her battle against one of life's cruelest diseases. It's a story of seemingly infinite compassion and devotion and of the power of love. Not only has Mariah become one of the longest-surviving victims of ALS in medical history, but also her life continues to be rich and productive. The quality of her work as a therapist, teacher, and healer continues to deepen.

When asked how she has managed to slow the deterioration from her disease, Mariah's eyes filled with tears. Turning toward her husband, she said, "It's him. He believes in the power of love to heal. He believes in me. Without Ron's continual, ongoing, loving support, I couldn't be doing what I'm doing now. I wouldn't even be alive today."

As he heard these words, Ron's eyes, too, filled with tears. "This isn't what either of us bargained for, but it's what we were given. Although I don't always do a great job of uncomplainingly accepting our reality, I do my best."

Ron's willingness to acknowledge his failure to bring as much grace as he would like to the challenges that he and Mariah share reflects his high standard of commitment. During the course of our interview, we lost our professional composure several times and were moved to tears at the almost indescribable expression of mutual love and devotion these two share. We could feel on a visceral level that their love heals not only each other but also all who enter into their presence. To be with them, as we were, for even a short time is truly a blessing. More than any other couple we spoke with, Mariah and Ron embody the notion that, when two hearts are separate, all difficulties can seem insurmountable, but when they are one, nothing is impossible.

MARIAH: I was the last of my group of friends to marry. My parents had had a painful divorce, which left me scared and distrustful. Both of my parents were severe alcoholics, and I was an only child in a strict Catholic family who considered divorce shameful. My father left the family when I was two and a half years old, and after that I had absolutely no contact with him — no visits, calls, letters, or birthday cards. My mother was so bitter that she wouldn't let him see me. It was only after he died that I found out he had kept tabs on me through his sister, my aunt Kay, and that his loss of me had been heartbreaking for him. Out of this trauma, I made up my mind that I would never get divorced. And one way to make certain I would never divorce was to not marry. I dated a lot, but I didn't trust men or myself.

RON: My parents didn't have a good marriage either. My father was an angry man, and he took out a lot of his anger on me. Growing up with verbal abuse didn't do a lot for my self-esteem, and I believed that if I ever did marry, I would be like my father and ruin my wife. I knew enough to realize that I had some work to do on myself to heal those inner wounds, and I got involved in personal growth and therapy. By age thirty-seven, I was finally beginning to realize I wasn't my father. Mariah and I met at a party, and from the beginning there was a strong power between us. She told me later that when I walked in the door she immediately told her girlfriend, "Leave him alone; he's mine." Standing next to her at the buffet table, the first thing I said to Mariah was "What are you doing here?" At that moment our arms were touching. She answered, "Right now I'm touching you." "Has anyone ever told you that you are manipulative?" I asked her. "Yes, they have," she said, "and I am." These two responses reflected two of Mariah's most fundamental values, unconditional honesty and awareness of present-moment experience, both of which are the core of her work as a gestalt therapist.

MARIAH: We courted for two years, and during that time we matured and really got to know each other. I saw essential goodness in Ron and could tell he had the right raw materials. I knew he would be a great father. To have a good father for my children was of utmost importance to me, because of my own absent father.

RON: There was something about Mariah that felt comfortable, stable, and exciting to me. I was absolutely clear that we were meant for each other. We were at the point where I was going to propose, when something came up that neither of us ever expected. It turned out to be a huge crisis, but at first it seemed like just a small physical problem. Her symptoms first appeared in the spring of 1981. Mariah was a serious racquetball player, and one day she found herself experiencing difficulty unclenching her grip from the handle of her racquet.

MARIAH: My fingers were twitching uncontrollably, and my hands were cramping. Something was clearly wrong, but I had no idea what it could be. I got a referral to a neurologist, who examined me and diagnosed me as having an inoperable brain tumor. We got the news on Ron's thirty-ninth birthday, June 30, 1981.

RON: We left the neurologist's office that day in a state of shock. I had been planning to propose to Mariah, and brain tumor or no brain tumor, I still intended to. This was the woman of my dreams, and I was intent on marrying her, no matter what.

MARIAH: That evening we went out to dinner, and Ron popped the question. We didn't have much money back then, and he proposed with a cigar band. I was of course deeply moved, but I told him, "Things have changed, Ron. I'm not who I was."

RON: She was giving me a graceful out, but I wouldn't even consider it. A few weeks later, we got a second opinion on her illness. Mariah was given a series of tests, and the results were conclusive. It was not a tumor. It was ALS. We were told what to expect regarding the progressive deterioration of the disease. Mariah's mind would remain clear, but she would lose control over her body, beginning with her extremities, hands and feet, and the paralysis would work its way up her body, affecting her ability to talk, eat, and eventually breathe. The doctor told us that, on average, ALS patients live for three to five years after the diagnosis. He gave Mariah a 10 percent chance of living two more years.

MARIAH: Both Ron and I really wanted to have children, but the doctor strongly advised against it. He claimed that pregnancy would greatly hasten the progression of the disease and would further weaken my body. After we left the doctor's office, we had a long talk. Once again I gave Ron an opportunity to reconsider the idea of getting married. I told him I would absolutely understand and wouldn't blame him if he chose not to go ahead with it.

RON: For the second time, I politely refused Mariah's offer to take a graceful out. I told her, "No, we're going through with the plans we made. We're going to get through this somehow, and you're going to be okay." We both agreed to go ahead and start a family despite the doctor's warnings.

"Sacred denial" can save your life

MARIAH: We practiced what I'd call "sacred denial." That is, we chose not to accept the prognosis and warnings as a reality set in stone, but rather as an opinion about something that might not come to pass. We knew there were variables in this equation we could influence, and that the medical statistics didn't consider some of those factors. We were determined to do everything within our power to slow the deterioration as much as possible.

Within three months of the diagnosis, we were married. I got pregnant on our wedding night. Nine months later, in July of 1982, we had our first child, Luke, a beautiful boy. I was in labor for thirty-one hours. Immediately after the birth, one of the nurses took the baby away to the nursery. We both wanted him to stay with us, and Ron insisted they bring our son back. When they refused, Ron said, "If you don't bring me our baby in five minutes, I'm going to the nursery and I'll take him myself." Less than five minutes later they brought him. That's only one of the many, many examples of how Ron has taken a stand for what is important to me and to us.

RON: Twenty-two months later we had our second son, Cole. We had planned two more children, but when Mariah noticed weakening in her left hand during the second pregnancy, we decided to stop. Mariah has been living with ALS for twenty-eight years now. During this time, she's maintained an active psychotherapy practice with individuals and groups, has given eight to ten workshops every year, and has a three-year Gestalt training program with thirty-five students. That's a lot of work, even for a person who doesn't have health issues.

MARIAH: I have defied the statistics, largely because of Ron. Our marriage is a major component of my health and my defiance of the odds. When I was initially diagnosed, I asked myself whether to believe the doctors or my husband who really knew me. I chose to believe Ron. He has always been utterly convinced that we could do this. I also rely on other means, such as prayer, exercise, supplements, the power of intention, and doing work I absolutely love. Being with my clients in such an intimate way gives me healing energy all the time. And my children have been an inspiration for me to stay alive and as healthy as possible. And on top of all I am doing to heal, I respect the mystery and stay in the question "Who knows?"

RON: A big part of my life has to do with taking care of Mariah. I'd like to say that I always love it, but the truth is I don't. However, my attitude is that this is my wife, I love her, and it's the right thing to do. In my life I have not always been a caregiver, but now I am one. The process hasn't been sudden. It's continued to unfold gradually and slowly. At first it was just a matter of "Could you button my shirt?" It was only one button; then it was all the buttons. Then it was brushing her teeth and dressing Mariah completely. Now she must lean on me, or someone, everywhere she walks. Her speech is sometimes difficult for new people to understand, so I must be her translator. I don't see it as noble. I'm sometimes angry at the disease and the relentless demands on me twenty-four/seven. I sometimes forget who I am; I have to stop and get back to myself. I replenish myself by doing things like playing my guitar and playing basketball, so I don't burn out. I probably need to do that more.

We can see our unacknowledged beauty and goodness reflected in the eyes of our beloved

MARIAH: I'm grateful that Ron sees me as a woman and a wife, and not a patient or an invalid. And he is always there, reliably generous, protective, and not a martyr. He speaks up when he's unhappy. When I was in the hospital with a systemic blood infection, he was there day and night to see to it that nothing went wrong. He slept on two chairs. He has this authentic optimism. His attitude is "We can handle this." His faith in my longevity is unshakable, and therefore I trust in his conviction when I have moments of doubt.

I am very dependent on Ron now. It is humbling for me. I'd always been such an independent woman. I sometimes feel guilty that I have ALS, but there are many fabulous lessons in surrendering to "thy will be done." I'm certain that I'm a better person for having ALS. My youthful arrogance went out the window long ago. I have a depth of patience and compassion that I would never have fathomed without my disease. Saint Augustine says that the reward of patience is patience. I know that my experience has enabled me to help people become more resilient themselves and to grow in their ability to deal with loss.

RON: Some time ago, I asked Mariah if, when she was diagnosed, she could have seen herself as she is today, she would have wanted to live. She told me she would have chosen to die. She wouldn't have wanted to be bent over and so dependent. But now we have created a very full life, full of love, friendships, travel, and rewarding work. We are husband and wife first and foremost. She has no self-pity. We both choose to look at the gifts we have, rather than what we don't have.

MARIAH: ALS has been a difficult teacher, and it quickly and relentlessly pushed us both to the heart of the matter. We have learned so much about what is necessary in order to shift and heal, and these are lessons I've been able to pass on to others. I know in my bones that there are infinite possibilities available to us when love and compassion are present, and that we always have the power to manifest them, regardless of our circumstances!

12.

A GENEROUS SPIRIT IS
ITS OWN REWARD

Tom and Nancy O'Neill

Tom O'Neill is a bear of a man, broad-shouldered, with a ruddy complexion and a large girth. He doesn't need much padding to fill out the Santa Claus costume he wears annually for his staff and their children. But it's not just Tom's appearance and his outfit that have earned him the nickname "Santa Claus." As the director of food concessions at the Squaw Valley Ski Resort in north Lake Tahoe, and a resident of the area for over thirty-five years, Tom has one of the most recognizable faces in the community. He is known for his extraordinary generosity to his community, his ever-present smile, and his contagious laughter. He's the kind of guy every man would like to call his best friend. And he absolutely adores Nancy.

Tom spent the first fourteen years of his life in New York City, the son of a fire chief and a homemaker, both strict Irish Catholics. Nancy is a Southern belle from Alabama who was the only member of her family to "escape" to California. Physically, Nancy is Tom's polar opposite: she is slight with delicate features. And they are as different temperamentally as they are physically. Where Tom tends to be abstract in his thinking, Nancy is specific and detail oriented. Tom has a laissez-faire attitude about child rearing. Nancy is concerned about limits. Tom sees nothing wrong with just getting by once in a while. Nancy expects A's of herself in everything she does. Tom always trusts that everything is going to work out. Nancy's not so sure.

Tom and Nancy are core members of the north Lake Tahoe community and have been mentors to hundreds of children and young people over the years. They exemplify a spirit of service that is inspiring and compelling, and they do it with a kind of ease and grace that makes it seem effortless. They would be the last people in the world to see themselves or what they do as being anything other than ordinary, and this humility and generosity of spirit makes them extraordinary. It's amazing what people can create together when they have no need to be special.

NANCY: I'm from Alabama, the Deep South. I grew up in the fifties in what I guess would be considered a very traditional family living in a very conservative community. My family was religious, strict Southern Baptist, judgmental of other religions and denominations that didn't agree with their interpretations of scripture. My older sister still lives in Alabama, as do almost all my relatives. I'm the one who "escaped." Most of my family thinks California is just too weird. When my aunt found out I was dating a man (Tom) who lived in California, she told me that, if you lifted up the entire U.S.A. and shook it, everything that was loose and wasn't "right" — an important word where I come from — would land in California.

TOM: I grew up in a Catholic family, very Catholic. I went to Catholic schools from kindergarten to college — I graduated from a Jesuit college in Santa Clara. My father was a chief in the fire department in Brooklyn, but when I was fourteen my family moved from New York to Arizona. I think the main reason was to get us kids into better schools. Education had a high value for my parents, right up there with religion. I always wanted to be a pilot, and after I graduated from college I enlisted in the navy, got into the pilot-training program, and went to Pensacola, Florida, for flight school. That's where I met Nancy. I was twenty-three when we met, and she was nineteen. I fell for her right away, but I think it was a little different for her.

NANCY: I was in dental hygiene school in Pensacola at the time, and my girlfriends and I used to hang out at the clubs on the beach because that was where the "top guns" used to go. One night I was at a party at a beach house with some of my girlfriends, and this big guy walked up to me and offered me a drink from his wine bag. Before I could even answer, he squirted me in the face with his wine. He laughed. He actually thought that was funny. My first impression of Tom was "What a jerk!"

Tom and I kept being thrown together because we hung out in the same crowd. I was dating a man named Keith at this time, who was also a navy pilot and a good friend of Tom's. One day I got a call telling me that Keith had been killed in a training accident. I was devastated, and so was Tom. He and I shared our grief over losing our friend, and it brought us closer together. I was impressed with Tom's tender heart.

TOM: Once I finished my training command and got my wings, I was transferred to a squadron in Brunswick, Maine. There was no way we were going to have a long-distance relationship. So in 1967, Nancy and I got married. At the end of my enlistment, I was offered a position as a pilot for Northwest Airlines. We were all set to move to Minnesota, where their headquarters was based, but just before the move I got a call from Northwest telling me the deal was off. Nancy and I had talked about wanting to live in California, and we both loved the outdoors in general. We knew that if we were ever going to live out our dreams, this would be the time to do it, so we decided to move to the West Coast. From the first day we arrived in Lake Tahoe, we've both been completely in love with this place. As far as we were concerned, we had found paradise.

NANCY: In 1975, our first son, Nick, was born, and five years later we had Matt. Matt has always been very much his own person. He marches to a different drummer. And while I appreciate and respect who he is, it hasn't always been easy for me to know how to best support him.

If it's to be, it's up to me

NANCY: I wanted to believe that the school system would provide the appropriate support for kids like Matt who needed something different from what was being offered. We recognized that the school's approach just didn't work, but it became increasingly apparent that the school board didn't see it that way. In fact, by the time Matt got into third grade, things on the board had taken a serious turn for the worse and were going in the opposite direction of what I believed kids needed.

I hated to admit it, but I knew that if there were going to be any changes, I was going to have to make them happen. With Tom's support and the encouragement of my friends, I made up my mind to run for a seat on the school board. It was a decision that would ultimately change my life.

Running for public office was the last thing I ever thought I would do. I'm a very shy person, and I had always been terrified of speaking in public. Two of my opponents were well known in the community. One was the pastor at the Episcopal church, who was also on the hospital board, and the other was the president of the chamber of commerce. When I met with the pastor and suggested that he drop out of the race, he laughed in my face. But the joke was on him. I ended up winning the election.

TOM: Nine months into her term of office, a religious fundamentalist group gathered enough signatures in their aggressive campaign to hold a recall election. Nancy was too progressive for them, and they were determined to get rid of her. Nancy's commitment pulled me in.

NANCY: Single-handedly, Tom raised enough money to hire an attorney who specialized in this kind of case. Tom exposed the extremist group to the community, including our neighbors who had previously supported the recall. He took on a leadership role and exposed the true motivation of this group, which in our view was not to enhance the quality of public education but to install their own narrow agenda.

TOM: By 80 percent of the vote, the recall was crushed. Nancy went on to serve on the school board for three consecutive terms. You better believe she got over her fear of public speaking! Her participation on the board completely transformed the quality of the local public school system.

Although I had always known that Nancy was plenty powerful, seeing her accomplishments this vividly was an epiphany for me. I saw the same light around Nancy that I had seen the day I met her. I learned an important lesson during this time: as a marriage matures, the key is to support each other's growth.

What you appreciate, appreciates

NANCY: Tom is not just respected but is also loved by everyone in the business where he works, from the dishwashers and hamburger flippers to the top-level managers. He approaches people with a level of caring and support that you just don't see much of these days. He sees them not simply as employees there to do a job but as unique, special individuals who deserve care, support, and respect. Tom's devotion to his staff and his deep generosity inspire a level of commitment and dedication from them in return. He shows his appreciation by rewarding them in countless ways, and the cycle continues.

Tom puts his money where his mouth is. He doesn't just talk about the importance of giving support and showing appreciation, he's continually involved in ventures that support local and national causes to serve the underprivileged and people in need in our community. Over the years he's raised hundreds of thousands of dollars for all kinds of causes, from multiple sclerosis to the humane society, and many more. Tom's enthusiasm and generosity are contagious and have infected almost all those around him with the joy of giving.

TOM: My life is so full; I just want to give a little back. Besides, I couldn't have done a lot of this without Nancy's support and belief in me. It was her conviction that I could do it that made it possible for me to take on something I never imagined I was suited for.

NANCY: When I was in my fifties, I finally decided to get a college degree. I'm a perfectionist in everything I do, and college has been no exception. I knew I had to complete raising my two sons before I could throw myself into my academic studies.

TOM: I have a different personality. My attitude is "C's earn degrees."

NANCY: Tom good-naturedly teases me for slaving over my papers, but I know he's proud of me for earning A's in all my courses. At times I'm stressed by the demands of my course work, but I maintain a standard of excellence. I derive a deep sense of satisfaction from the sense of mastery that comes with thoroughly learning the subject matter, even in courses that are not in my area of interest. I am ecstatic to be finally, at this late stage in life, fulfilling my dream — earning a degree — and it has given me an enhanced sense of who I am.

Great marriages thrive with great friendships

NANCY: My friends are crucial to my well-being. For me, friendships outside the marriage are not a luxury, they are a necessity. Having this outside support takes a lot of pressure off Tom. If I don't have strong support from my women friends, I'm inclined to turn to him for things he may not be able to give me at that particular time. My closest friends and I have agreed to challenge each other, in caring ways, to live our lives more consciously and responsibly.

TOM: I love it that Nancy has so many great friends. The connections we each have with other people have allowed us to accept change, which has been important to the well-being of our relationship. Since things are always in flux, we realized that we might as well embrace change. Change allows new doors to open and puts us on another path on which to learn and grow.

NANCY: What I love the most about Tom is his stability. He's as sturdy as a rock. I also appreciate his ability to be with people in a way that allows them to be who they are. This is one of the qualities that make him such a good father: he lets our two sons just be themselves. I don't think he has a controlling bone in his body.

TOM: Many years ago there was a pivotal moment in our life together when Nancy said to me, "This marriage may be working for you, but it's not working for me." It was the beginning of a series of conversations that required me to show up more in our marriage. I remember it so clearly because it was a major turning point and deepened our connection. One thing I can always count on is that Nancy will tell me the truth. It's not always easy for me to hear, but I always appreciate it in the end.

NANCY: We have realized over the years that a deep relationship requires small acts of kindness and courtesy. We have learned to never underestimate the value of these small gestures. Some people are blessed with great marriages. Some have great friendships. I have both. I feel like I hit the jackpot!

13.

A PAINFUL PAST CAN OPEN THE DOOR TO THE DEEPEST LOVE

Joseph and Robyn Whyte (not their real names)

Robyn and Joseph's story stands out as a profound example of the human capacity to overcome extreme adversity. It illuminates the potential of loving partnerships to heal even the most painful and damaging childhood wounds through loving and trustworthy contact. Joseph and Robyn came from worlds that couldn't have been more disparate. But while there was little common ground in the outer aspects of their lives, their driving passion for intimate connection proved to be more powerful than all their differences put together. A series of serendipitous meetings thrust them into each other's lives in ways that could make even the greatest skeptic a believer in divine intervention. Regardless of what forces brought these two together, their story exemplifies what can happen when two people choose to bring love, authenticity, and passion into their lives.

Robyn and Joseph didn't simply luck into an ideal relationship; they cultivated it by doing the work necessary to create the connection their hearts longed for. As it turned out, the work they each had to do to heal their own wounds was also the same work needed to create a loving marriage. Like many of the couples described here, they found that falling in love isn't the end of the rainbow. It's the beginning of the yellow brick road, which, as we know, is fraught with challenge, surprise, adventure, and peril. Committed relationships are not for the faint of heart. They often entail grappling with memories buried in the depths of our own consciousness, which intimate connections reawaken.

The line between our deepest longings and our greatest fears can be very fine. As this couple discovered, it takes more than love and desire to fuel the process of relationship. Without courage, commitment, creativity, and a healthy helping of playfulness to keep things from getting too serious, dreams of lifelong fulfillment are not likely to be realized. Joseph and Robyn have realized their dreams, and then some. They found that sometimes the biggest risk we have to take is to embrace a dream that seems impossible or inappropriate. As the bumper sticker says, "Miracles happen."

JOSEPH: I was the first child of two working-class parents who were barely out of their teens when I was born. My parents provided for the family through thievery and petty crime. It was part of a long tradition that had been handed down on both sides of the family for generations. The home I was born into, in 1943, was in the heart of an inner-city slum. The fact that I was born at all is a minor miracle, because my mother, distressed by the pregnancy and unmarried at the time, made a strenuous attempt to abort me. My parents married shortly before the birth of my younger sister, but separated and divorced not long after the marriage. At the age of five, I was sent to live with my mother's parents, who were primitive and brutal.

We lived in two dark, small rooms. There was no running water. For a toilet, we all used a single pot, which stood at the end of the bed. In the winter, the only source of heat we had at night was our two dogs, who would sleep with us. There was no heat because my grandparents didn't want to "waste" the precious coal at night. I never saw a toothbrush. What I remember most vividly is the stench of the place, the smell of rat feces in the walls, the overflowing chamber pot, and the smell of stale human sweat.

The houses on the block were ramshackle and run down, and they were gradually being demolished. Our home was the last standing, and the rats from the other buildings all descended on ours. The noise from the rats gnawing in the walls was so loud we couldn't hear the radio. My grandparents' fighting was relentless. They didn't speak to each other; they just raged continually. On one occasion, in a fit of drunken rage, my grandfather hurled a heavy iron pot in my direction because I was being "too noisy." The pot missed my head by inches and left a hole in the wall. Either one of them could turn in a flash and become violent. It was totally unpredictable; I never knew when the next blow would be struck. I lived in a constant state of tension, and realized I had to get out of there if I was to survive. I think I was about ten at the time.

Petty criminality, too, was part of my everyday reality. My grandparents started involving me when I was five years old. My grandmother used to send me to place illegal gambling bets. No one told me it was illegal, but even as a small boy I sensed that what I was doing wasn't right.

I did escape when I was thirteen and went to live with a family of a classmate. I eventually lived with three different families before graduating from high school. What I endured as a child left me with a deep longing, a hunger, to find peace and love in my life. I grew up with a desperate desire to have a marriage and family that were the opposite of what I witnessed as a child. Out of my experience I have learned that you're not necessarily doomed to repeat the same old family patterns. But in order for me to break free from them, I had to feel the pain and grieve the loss that characterized so much of my life. Never a day goes by that I don't feel blessed and filled with gratitude.

The "good life" can't fill an empty heart

ROBYN: We had both been married before. I had been married sixteen years and Joseph twenty. In my early twenties I had married the "right" man: John was conservative, his background and religion were similar to mine, and he had great career potential. He was everything I had grown up expecting a husband to be. Together we founded and managed a business that became extremely successful. We shared a lavish and luxurious lifestyle, taking a lot of vacation time every year and traveling around the world. We ate at the finest restaurants, traveled first class, and enjoyed the good life.

I was one of perhaps very few twenty-three-year-old virgins in the country at the time I got married. Even as sexually inexperienced as I was, I grew suspicious on our honeymoon that something was wrong. The sex wasn't very good, and it never really got any better. Since the business was so successful, we had plenty of money, so when I suggested we go to a sex therapist, we were able to afford the one who got the highest recommendation. He gave us a pornographic movie to watch, which didn't work for either of us. We never did get any help with our lack of emotional intimacy.

We were both so busy running our business, creating the "perfect life" together, that we forgot to tend the heart of our relationship. While we were building our life together, neither of us noticed what was missing, or maybe we were just willing to accept life as it was. Over time, it became increasingly difficult for me to tolerate the pain of our disconnection. John wasn't bothered by it, or at least he didn't seem to be. We both came from families where you didn't talk about these things.

Eventually I initiated a divorce. John resisted it, and things got ugly. The divorce settlement was a costly, painful, drawn-out ordeal. Both of our families were distressed and appalled, and I was perceived as the cause of the breakup. Our families were extremely concerned with appearances, but I only cared about leaving a marriage I felt was unfulfilling. I didn't care what people thought. I needed to find what was missing in my life. When the divorce was over, I went traveling.

Not every marriage can be saved

JOSEPH: When Robyn and I first met, she had just gotten out of an unfulfilling marriage, and I was still in one. My ex-wife and I had many good years together, but the final few were emotionally barren. While Robyn and her husband had not gone to great lengths to save their marriage, that was not the case with Anna and me. We spent a huge amount of time and money in therapy trying to resuscitate what felt like a relationship made of love and pain. It wasn't for lack of trying that our marriage collapsed. I loved my wife; I loved my work; I loved my daughters; I really loved being in a family. What I hated was my frustration at not being emotionally close to my wife. It wasn't her fault. We were both still caught up in old patterns we'd learned from our families. Neither of us had had much experience being emotionally intimate. We both wanted it, but we were unable to connect.

ROBYN: Joseph and I experienced a strong attraction to each other when we first met. We didn't act on it at first, and when we said goodbye, neither of us expected to see the other again. Over the course of the next several years, we had a few more unintended meetings.

JOSEPH: The last time we ran into each other, I knew there was a reason for it. By this time, my marriage was all but over. My children were grown and no longer living at home, and the emotional gap between my wife and myself was huge. I knew I would have to leave, even though the thought of it filled me with grief and fear. When Robyn and I ran into each other that last time, I immediately experienced an unmistakable message in my body telling me that I had to be with her. The pull was overwhelming. I felt elation, fear, and sadness simultaneously. On the one hand, I knew I could not say "no" to the deep longing I felt in my heart. On the other hand, I had never been unfaithful to my wife, Anna. It had not been part of my plans to have an affair while I was still married, but from the instant Robyn touched me it was electric. It was everything I had wanted to feel in my marriage but never had. In the end, my heart won out. After spending a few days with Robyn, I knew for sure that this was what I had been craving.

I told Robyn when I left that I would come back after I had settled things with my family, but we both knew there was no guarantee that I would stick to my guns. It was one thing to fall in love with someone, and another to end a long-term marriage and break up a family. I knew it was what I wanted, but I wasn't sure I'd find the strength to do it.

The next few months proved to be one of the most painful times of my life. Upon my return home, I acknowledged my relationship with Robyn to Anna and informed her of my decision to seek a divorce. Leaving the family was the hardest part. Even though my marriage had been emotionally unfulfilling, and my daughters had grown and moved out of the house, we had all been very close, a very tight unit, for years. The thought of leaving everyone was overwhelming. Both Anna and I still cared very deeply for each other, and that made things even harder. She was hurt, but the pain of years of unsuccessfully trying to breathe life into the marriage had taken a toll on her, too, and she knew that, as painful as divorce was, it was probably best for us both.

I returned to Robyn with two suitcases containing some clothes and a few other possessions. I had given away or sold practically everything else I owned, or left it in what was now Anna's home. I came back to Robyn starting from scratch. No home, no job, no family, and no idea of whether we would be able to make it work. All I knew was that I loved Robyn and was willing to take a risk.

ROBYN: For the first time in my life, I'd had a taste of what it felt like to really love and be loved by someone. I didn't know what the future held, but I knew that my life had to include Joseph. There was so much about him that I loved. What I think I found most attractive about him was his nonjudgmental nature. I felt so accepted. From the beginning, I'd always felt like I could be myself, even my not-so-lovable self. His love and acceptance helped me love and accept myself. But despite the love we have for each other, we've had our share of difficulties like any other couple. It hasn't been perfect bliss all the time; I don't think it is for anyone.

Emotional and sexual intimacy are cornerstones of a great marriage

ROBYN: In the beginning, we were deliriously in love and very sexual. I had spent so many years sexually deprived that I was making up for lost time. Joseph was such a connector; he loved being close all the time. After a while, I began to feel overwhelmed by so much contact. I was saturated. At first we didn't have the words to describe what we were experiencing, but we stayed with the challenge and finally found them. I told him that I felt invaded, and Joseph told me that when I pulled away after being so close, he felt abandoned. I kept telling him it was just too much for me, and I asked him to give me a little time to "grow a bigger container." What I meant was that I needed to learn how to enjoy that much attention and closeness.

JOSEPH: When we first moved in together, our home was a tiny one-room cabin by a lake in a remote region. We lived there for about three years, and at times it felt like we were living in a pressure cooker. There was nowhere to go that was out of the sight of the other person. Whenever we were angry, we had to go around each other, averting our eyes, circulating in that one room. We had to learn to be with each other when we were at our worst.

Things came to a head one day when we had a bad argument. Robyn was in such a fury that she left the cabin and moved into a girlfriend's house to sort things out. She was gone for two and a half days and didn't call me. She had never done anything like that before, and I was hurt, frightened, and outraged, all at once. In my mind, I was saying things like "She's punishing me and withholding her love. I can't trust her because she is too controlling." I noticed these condemning thoughts going through my mind, and caught myself being carried away by this sweep of character assassination. I said to myself, "Hold on a minute here. She doesn't get to dictate whether I trust her or not. That's my decision."

After I reminded myself of Robyn's lovely qualities, I felt my tension start to ebb away and my personal power coming back. My tight chest started to relax, and I felt softness around my heart that had been missing for days. Twenty-five minutes after this turnaround, she walked in the door, ready to talk.

"What can I do differently?" is a better question than "How can I get her to change?"

ROBYN: I'd had a complete meltdown at my girlfriend's house and had been feeling terrible. I'd also begun thinking about Joseph's positive qualities, the things about him that I loved. My feelings were too strong to share with him on the phone. I had to tell him in person. As painful as that brief separation was, it was necessary and helped bring us together. It gave us a chance to disengage from our reactive patterns and remember what we loved about each other.

We realized that whenever we tried to communicate while possessed by intense feelings, the situation would inevitably deteriorate and our emotions would become inflamed. We saw that we just couldn't talk to each other when we were in such a state of mind. We had to calm our own minds before we could have a productive conversation. If we didn't, it would just be more of the same old attack-and-defend.

JOSEPH: We had to learn how to look at ourselves and deal with our own feelings, rather than indulge our impulses to control each other. We were better at this sometimes than at other times.

ROBYN: There was a ghastly cycle that we frequently got caught in. I would fall into a hole so deep that it felt like I couldn't come back. I would go down the chute. When I went into my own world to soothe myself, this activated Joseph's fear of losing me, which would prompt him to rush in and try to bring me back. Then I would feel totally invaded, and I'd react by pulling back. Then he'd try again to bring me back. This mutually reinforcing cycle would eventually deteriorate to the point where one or both of us would become overwhelmed with feelings of fear, pain, or anger. We knew that we had to learn how to deal with these cycles in order to continue to live with each other. We had to learn to do something different.

JOSEPH: I had to experience my discomfort without speaking. I had to contain my feelings and opinions instead of blurting them out. One of the things I noticed when we disengaged was that there was a lawyer in my mind who was always building a very strong case about what was wrong with Robyn. I learned that I couldn't shut him up, but I didn't have to share his opinions with her. I let the lawyer run his mouth off to me, but not to her. After a while he began to quiet down. When I was able to cool down a bit and look more clearly within myself, I could come back to Robyn with an open heart and a greater ability to really listen to her. My body would tell me when I was ready to reconnect. I would notice that, when I looked at her, she was no longer offensive to my eyes.

ROBYN: When Joseph would make an overture to reconnect with me, I was always glad to feel him coming into my presence. But I wasn't always ready for him.

JOSEPH: I had to learn not to take this as a personal rejection and trust that, in time, Robyn would be ready. Eventually, she always was.

ROBYN: There was enough goodwill that I knew I could ask for a little more time to get myself ready if I needed it.

JOSEPH: Then when Robyn would finally come to me and say she was ready, those words were like the voices of angels to my ears. Living in the cabin was like living in an ongoing intensive relationship workshop. Our close quarters and limited resources continually posed new challenges for us. We owned only one car, and Robyn used it every day to go to work, leaving me alone in the cabin all day. For the first few months, I didn't have a job. I just spent the day by myself at home doing chores, chopping wood, and taking care of the homestead. I enjoyed the beauty of the woods, but by the end of the day I was lonely for Robyn. I would watch the clock, waiting for her to come home. One day a week, she would stop to buy the week's groceries after work. On those days, the wait often felt unbearable. When she would finally come home, I would be like an excited puppy.

ROBYN: I would come into the house after a busy day at work with a week's supply of groceries, exhausted and needing some space to myself. I generally forced myself to engage with Joseph, even though I usually didn't feel like it. He didn't get it that I really needed to decompress for a while, and I wouldn't tell him. He would keep talking, and wanted to kiss and hug me, and I just wasn't ready for all that. Eventually, I would get angry at him.

JOSEPH: As soon as Robyn would raise her voice, I would immediately feel like that scared, abandoned little boy whose parents didn't want him. I would react by trying even harder to reengage her, hoping to bring her back. Of course, this would just make things worse. After one particularly painful interchange, I finally had the presence of mind to ask, "What is it you really want?"

ROBYN: I told him, "I've worked all day and gone all over town shopping. I'm stressed out. I love it that you greet me and welcome me and hug me hello. But one kiss and hug are enough. Help me bring the groceries in and let me put them away by myself. When I'm ready, I'll come and get you."

JOSEPH: The next time she came home, I followed her instructions to the letter. When she was ready, Robyn came and sat down quietly beside me and put her arm around my shoulder. I yelled out "hooray." For me it's like the old cowboy movies I used to watch when I was a child. Hostile Indians would surround the wagon train; the music would change, and the cavalry would come charging in. The pioneers would know they were saved and yell "hooray." Part of me felt that Robyn had saved me. That was the last time we played out that pattern. Now we have a tradition: whoever comes home first gets an exuberant greeting of "hooray" from the other. And it feels just as good hearing Robyn call it out as it does when I do it!

We've created a number of rituals and practices intended to deepen the quality of our connection. For example, we've made Saturday the most important day of the week. We hold the entire day open. We don't answer the phone, and we don't spend any part of that day with other people. Everything we do that day is foreplay, setting the mood for lovemaking. We never have sex; we only make love. We know all week long that we will make love on Saturday. Sometimes I say to Robyn during the week, "Is it Saturday yet?"

When Saturday comes, we begin the day by cuddling in bed and reflecting on the previous week. Sometimes I read poetry aloud, and we often play a rhyming word game we made up that inevitably ends with us breaking up in laughter.

ROBYN: After we make love, we often go for a hike in nature. We love the beauty of the plants, trees, and water that is all around where we live. Everything inspires us because we are wide open and available. Even the mundane things take on a special luster. There's a never-ending freshness to our relationship that hasn't yet ceased to thrill us.

JOSEPH: We've both come to understand how sensitive each of us is, and to appreciate what a gift that sensitivity is. It's the depth of our feelings for each other that has allowed our love to grow and us to heal. I can't imagine any more blessed work than that of creating a loving relationship.

14.

THE PLAY OF MARRIAGE
HAS MANY CHARACTERS

Hal and Sidra Stone

When Hal and Sidra Stone first met, getting into a new relationship was the last thing on their minds. Hal was a Jungian analyst who practiced and taught and kept a full schedule. Sidra, a practicing psychotherapist, was interested in learning about symbolic visualization. Hal was known as a leading expert in the field. Both he and Sidra were married to other people at the time.

What began as a working relationship between a student and teacher became, within a few weeks, a cocreative venture, and Hal and Sidra developed a process in which they were alternately each other's teacher. They facilitated an experience of deep inquiry that revealed hidden aspects of their personalities, illuminating their inner unconscious selves and bringing them to consciousness far more effectively than any of the traditional models of psychotherapy they had previously experienced. This treatment model would eventually transform the orientation of psychotherapists throughout the world and the lives of thousands of people.

The process was immeasurably deepened because of the differences in their personalities and individual temperaments. Hal, a self-described introvert and spiritually oriented intellectual, lived in a world of ideas, concepts, and intuition. Sidra, a pragmatic, achievement-oriented extrovert, saw the world through the lens of behavioral psychology, where what matters most is the logic of rewards and punishments and solutions and explanations.

What's most impressive about Hal and Sidra isn't the great body of work they have created together, or the many books they have coauthored, or their international reputation as originators of the Voice Dialogue method of psychotherapy. It's their extraordinary relationship and the fact that, at the ages of seventy-one and eighty-one, they are more open, curious, adventurous, and passionate than ever. Their lives and their relationship embody the essential message that permeates all their teachings: that human beings can experience increased joy and fulfillment as they age, even into their ninth decade, and that learning and adventure can be an exhilarating, lifelong journey.

SIDRA: At the time I met Hal, I was a clinical psychologist practicing in Los Angeles. I was interested in receiving training to facilitate active-imagination and guided-imagery work. I called Hal's office and scheduled a series of training sessions. As soon as I got off the phone, I had a sense that this would be a fateful meeting, that something big was going to come from it.

HAL: My first meeting with Sidra was entirely clinical. We spoke briefly, and then I set the stage for her to enter a state of deep relaxation that is necessary to engage the part of the psyche that activates imagery and imagination. Almost immediately it became obvious to me that things weren't working. Rather than becoming more relaxed, Sidra was becoming increasingly more tense and resistant. I assured her that I wasn't a predator and had no sexual designs on her. She then allowed herself to go into a state of deep relaxation and emotional openness.

SIDRA: The day after the session, I had a dream that Hal and I were on a sailing vessel, and a voice instructed us not to stop anywhere for more than one night. We have come to understand the message of that dream as an injunction to keep going. That guideline has informed our relationship ever since. If we get into difficulty, we move into it, and through it, immediately.

HAL: By the fifth session, it had become obvious to me that we could no longer maintain the original structure of our relationship. It was no longer one of teacher and student; we were each other's teacher and student, and although there wasn't a physical element to our relationship, we were each obviously becoming deeply emotionally involved with the other. I knew by then that I was deeply in love with Sidra. I told her I wanted to change our contract from that of mentor and student to an agreement between two colleagues working supportively with each other. At this point, I was still very clear that I did not want to become romantically involved with Sidra.

SIDRA: We continued to work together in a format that was different from anything either of us had experienced. We weren't just discussing concepts intellectually; we were experiencing them. One day, Hal suggested that, rather than talk about vulnerability, I should become it. And so I did. I sat down on the floor. I let myself go completely. I immediately had the feeling of being Alice in Wonderland, going down the rabbit hole. I was no longer Sidra; I became a preverbal child, acutely sensitive to everything around me.

HAL: I had been doing this work for a while, but it had never been anything like this before. We began to identify and recognize different selves that exist within each of us. We spent the next five years identifying this amazing cast of characters, and the work we did together at this time informed and shaped our professions and provided a foundation for all the work we have done since.

We discovered that each self had a different history, a different way of perceiving the world, and a different physical expression. We gave them names such as the pusher, the inner critic, or the pleaser. They all demand a say in regard to our behaviors and life choices. We discovered that our lives and relationships began to transform as these parts were brought to consciousness and given expression.

SIDRA: During the course of our first years together, we each got a divorce. This was an intense and difficult time for each of us and for our families. Along with the fascinating explorations, the amazing discoveries, and the excitement of the expansion we felt, we experienced the loss of all we had known and depended on. We felt intense pain over the disruption we were causing the families we truly loved. In an attempt to properly honor our previous lives, and to give our children the opportunity to adjust to this new and, for them, uncomfortable situation, we postponed our marriage for some time. This was a good decision and helped ease the transition.

When we married and our relationship entered a whole new phase, in which we found ourselves calling each other by the names of our former spouses, we saw patterns from our previous marriages reemerge. This was a surprise to us, even though intellectually we knew that changing marriage partners doesn't change relationship patterns. We discovered a phenomenon that we came to call "bonding patterns," which are what we think of as the "default settings" for relationships. At these times, Hal and I would relate to each other as mother/son and father/daughter.

After we got married, these patterns became much stronger, as did the intensity of the emotions they generated in each of us. We saw that these patterns were not personal or unique to us, but universal. We wanted to develop a system that would enable us to work with our patterns in order to help other couples, but the truth of the matter is that our motivation was also selfish.

Your partner is your mirror, who reflects back both your attractive and unattractive parts

HAL: We discovered that the stronger our response was to each other's behavior, the more likely it was a reaction to a disowned part of our self. We found that, when we were able to give that self a voice for self-expression, everything shifted and opened up. But we had to be able to tell the truth to ourselves about what we were actually feeling, no matter what it was. One of the things I became aware of in looking at my reactions to Sidra was how frequently I found myself judging her. In examining this, I came to see that, whenever we had competing desires, I judged Sidra as being selfish or wrong in some way. I saw that my judgments were actually a key to discovering what I wanted at the time. If I judged her as lazy, it was usually because I felt overworked and unwilling to give myself the downtime she was taking. If I judged her as self-absorbed or self-indulgent, it was probably a result of my having failed to take care of myself.

SIDRA: For example, one morning when I was busily hunched over the keyboard, I looked out the window and noticed Hal feeding the deer. He loves doing this, and I could see how much he was enjoying himself. I suddenly became aware that I was grinding my teeth. My thought was "He's doing just what he feels like while I'm in here working." I saw that this feeling of resentment and envy illuminated an unacknowledged need to feel free to be myself and do those things that please me. I learned to look for the gift in every judgment.

Two people can be connected on different continents and separate in the same bed

HAL: We realized that what's most important in our connection is not what we're doing with or saying to each other, or even where we are physically in relationship to each other. What matters most is the quality of the energy between us. We've both become more cognizant of that connection when it's present and when it's not.

SIDRA: It's not a function of geography or emotions or behavior. It has to do with our consciousness of each other at any given moment. When we are energetically connected, the world is a lovely place. When we're not, the world feels dry and barren. We've found that we can be linked even at a distance, even when we're on different sides of the world. Conversely, we may not have it even if we're sitting in the same room.

The best way to avoid divorce is to have a no-fault marriage

SIDRA: When our connection is temporarily interrupted, we each must take responsibility for restoring it, rather than blaming the other person for the break or trying to get him or her to repair it. The basic premise of what we call a "no-fault" relationship is that each of us is accountable for our role. This is quite different from being responsible for the relationship. Among other things, we are required to feel the pain of the separation when it happens — to experience our own vulnerability — and to share this with the other. Often Hal is better able to start this conversation than I am, even though I, too, feel the intense pain of the separation. I am grateful that he can do this and does not keep track of whose turn it is to identify the disconnection.

HAL: Another situation occurred when we gave our attention to Sidra's children or grandchildren for a prolonged period of time. I would at first feel a vague sense of general upset. Then I would become judgmental of Sidra, assessing her as neglectful or selfish. Then if I stayed with my feeling, I would notice that there was jealousy underneath the judgments. Once it became clear to me that jealousy was an indicator that I wanted a better connection with Sidra, I was able to express my feelings and desires without making her or myself seem wrong, and we could recommit to our connection. But I had to get to the point where I was able to actually recognize what I was feeling and to express my needs and intention in a responsible way.

SIDRA: Sometimes I would sense that Hal was attracted to another woman, and the connection to her was getting stronger than was comfortable for me. During these times, I needed to be aware of my own vulnerability and to bring it into my connection with Hal without making him responsible for meeting my needs. My vulnerability is usually directly beneath my judgment. This isn't always a pretty picture, and often I pass through a fair amount of anger and judgment before getting to the vulnerability. Sometimes it was evident that the woman represented one of my disowned selves, or that she carried a self that was disowned by both Hal and me that needed to be better integrated into our lives. Invariably, the attraction pointed to a lack of balance — a lesson for me, or for us, to learn.

HAL: When I was younger, I lived much more in my head than in my heart or soul. Sidra has helped me find my heart, and our relationship has been my recent spiritual path. Both heart and spirit are now more fully integrated into my being, and I am no longer dependent on her, or the relationship, to bring those parts of myself into my life experience. I now own them and carry them myself.

SIDRA: I've always known that relationship is my spiritual path. The spiritual energy inherent in a deep personal connection has always been apparent to me. I've heard of an African tribe in which community members each receive their own special song, a song that is sung to them in the womb, at birth, at the significant times during their lifetimes, and finally at their deaths. My relationship with Hal has taught me to recognize my own song, and Hal has always encouraged me to sing it. When we are energetically connected at the deepest levels, I feel connected to the whole universe. In those moments there is no separation anywhere. Whether I'm caring for a grandchild, making coffee, cleaning the house, or writing a book, it's all the same. When we are connected in this way, we both live in a state of peace and grace. Of course we still have those moments when the selves take over; they want to speak out or act out, but we know how to deal with them much more quickly these days. Mostly we enjoy our lives and our relationship immensely.

Love isn't enough

HAL: When people ask me what advice I would give to a newly married couple, I say: "A marriage needs two people who love each other. Love, however, is not enough. What is essential for a rich and satisfying relationship is the initiation of the process of personal growth, of consciousness exploration, both individually and as a couple, so that there is a framework for dealing with the difficulties that life invariably brings. As you take your vows and make a commitment to the relationship, know that you are also beginning a journey of individual and coexploration that will go on forever and ever and ever."

SIDRA: The best advice I can give is: "Respect one another and re-spect your relationship, the best teachers you will ever receive. Do not try to fix each other. Instead, look for the lessons that are there to be learned from each other. Be accountable for who you are and for what you contribute to your relationship, including your negativity, your need for power or control, and other less-than-stellar contributions. All this is important; all this is part of the teaching.

"Trying to have the perfect relationship, or trying to fix things too soon, doesn't work. Relationship is not always an easy path, and there are no shortcuts. If you use your relationship as a mirror in which to view yourself clearly, it will show you your next step. Learning from what you see in this mirror will keep your life together an exciting and unpredictable journey, and it will, in the end, enable each of you to sing your own song, the song you were always meant to sing."

15.

IT'S NOT DESPITE OUR DIFFERENCES THAT WE CAN DEEPLY LOVE, IT'S BECAUSE OF THEM

Veda Lewis and Kathy Anastad

Kathy and Veda are a wholesome, all-American couple. They are clean livers. They don't swear, drink, smoke, or use drugs. They are pillars of their church and rarely miss a service. They are deeply family-oriented with strong traditional family values. They both love to watch and play sports. They are middle class in every way, and they are gay and biracial.

The two were initially brought together by their shared love of fencing, which proved to be the first of many interests and activities shared during their thirty years together in a committed partnership. But despite the many common aspects of their lives, there are some significant differences in their personalities and many of their views, ideas, desires, and even values. Kathy always wanted children; Veda did not. Kathy tends to jump into things; Veda is a planner. Veda's job is in Sacramento, California; Kathy works in Sonoma. Kathy comes from a Midwest Scandinavian heritage; Veda is African American. Veda is a homebody; Kathy loves to travel. Veda tends to be the serious type; Kathy loves to play. Kathy is touchy-feely; Veda is more formal.

Yet despite their differences, or perhaps because of them, Kathy and Veda have created a loving and enduring relationship that has far surpassed the dreams and expectations of either of them. In addition to the ordinary relationship challenges that most couples face, these two have the challenge of being a gay, mixed-race couple living in a family-oriented, mainstream American community. Their story illuminates the power and strength that can be found in sharing the deeper aspects of relationship, and how love, respect, and appreciation trump differences every time.

KATHY: I fell in love with Veda even before I met her. Just before meeting her, I had a sense that something important was about to happen in my life. We met in 1977, when I was out of college and she was in graduate school studying marine biology. At the time, I was heavily into fencing. One afternoon I drove over to Veda's apartment to pick up her roommate, who was also a fencer. We were going to a tournament. I saw Veda and felt an immediate and powerful attraction — I knew there was something very strong between us.

VEDA: I was taking fencing classes at San Francisco State University. I was just a beginner, but Kathy was great. I had heard about her: she had a reputation as being the best. Shortly after we met, I went to see her fencing in a tournament and was blown away. She seemed so relaxed and laid back, but when she was fencing it was almost like another personality took over. I remember thinking, "Whoa! This girl is really something!"

KATHY: I got into fencing in high school and really liked it, and when I went to college and tried out for the team, I made it. In my early twenties, I was trying to be heterosexual by being with a man — I wasn't ready to face the fact that I was gay. It was a slow process for me, and over time the truth became clearer to me. Still, it terrified me to imagine what my parents would think, how they would react to the news. My friends knew before I could admit it to myself. It took Veda's two roommates to finally convince me that Veda was interested in me in a romantic way. I'm really glad that Veda didn't give up.

VEDA: I've been clear about being a lesbian from a pretty early age. I had been on a couple of dates with guys in high school and recognized quickly that dating men wasn't for me. I didn't come out in high school, but I knew I was different. When I got to college, I went to a counselor at San Francisco State, which is probably the best school in the world to be in if you're coming out! She really helped me become clear about my sexual identity. I never felt that I had to repress my homosexuality, but I didn't get into a relationship right away. In fact, my relationship with Kathy is the only one I've ever had.

My mother didn't get angry with me when I came out, but she didn't really understand what I was experiencing. She thought I wanted to become a man. I explained that that wasn't the case, that I didn't want to change my gender and was not considering a sex change operation. This seemed to reassure her. She recovered from the shock pretty quickly, and we were soon back on loving terms again.

Love sometimes requires you to risk family disapproval

KATHY: My mother reacted a little differently when she found out about me. One day when I was visiting my family, she made a comment about the amount of time Veda and I were spending together, and she asked me if I was gay. "Yes," I said, "I am." She literally couldn't hear my answer, and so she asked me again. Once again I said, "Yes." The second time she heard me, and she just lost it. She completely fell apart. My mother had seven kids and serious expectations for each one of us. The girls were all supposed to marry and have children, and my being a lesbian did not in any way fit into her plan. She was both devastated and enraged, and she said some horrible things to me that I can't repeat. I was trying my best not to lose it and to keep our connection open, but nothing I said seemed to get through to her. I told her, "Mom, I'm no different than I was a minute ago. I'm the same Kathy who's always been your daughter." But she was deaf to it all.

My mom went off to her room, and a short time later my dad, who was a physician, came home after making his rounds at the hospital. He saw how upset I was, and he asked me what was wrong. I explained to him what had happened. He took a moment to take it in, and his reaction was completely different from my mom's. When he finally spoke, he said, "It's going to take a while for your mother to be able to deal with this. She can't hear you now, and you're going to have to wait until she can." He wasn't at all angry or emotional. He was very supportive and has been since that day. He said to me, "Just remember your mother is hurt now and unable to hear whatever you have to say. Time will help."

Sure enough, my dad was right. My mom and I didn't speak for exactly one year, and during that time she and I were completely disconnected. It was a painful position to be in, and as much as I have always loved my mother and always wanted us to be close, I couldn't bear the thought of not having Veda in my life. After a year, my mother and I began to communicate again, and we began the process of reconciliation. It's been almost thirty years that Veda and I have been together, and now my mother loves her.

VEDA: And I love her too. She initially thought I was an evil person who had corrupted her daughter. Kathy and I came through it with much deeper love and respect for each other than we had before. By the time Kathy came out to her family, we were already so deeply in love that there was no question that we would stay together.

KATHY: Many years after that break in my relationship with my mother, she explained that the shock of my gay lifestyle choice had been bad enough, but that the bigger issue for her was that the partner I chose was black. When she came out with that remark, it was a total shock to me. I had never been aware of my mother's racism. Both of my parents were born and raised in Minnesota, and my mother probably had never had any experience with black people while growing up.

What's fascinating to me, and what makes sense when you think about it, is that it wasn't until my mother got to know Veda, her parents, and her family that her biases started to break down. All the old myths crumbled. She saw how devoted everyone in Veda's family was to each other, how much they valued education, work, church, and spending time with one another, and how they accepted and appreciated diversity.

It was very different with my dad. He practiced medicine in San Francisco, and so he had a diverse patient clientele — rich, poor, black, white, Asian, Latino, gay, straight — and he treated them all equally. It took years for my mom to come around, but after she got to know Veda and her family, her bigotry started to subside.

In forgoing what we want, we may receive gifts we never expected

KATHY: I really love kids, but I knew Veda didn't want to have any. She had been responsible from an early age for the care of her younger brother and sister while her mother was working. I knew where Veda stood on being a parent, and I didn't want to put pressure on her. It was a huge issue for me — I had always wanted children of my own, so it was a tough position for me to be in. I ultimately decided that I would get involved with my siblings' children and be the best auntie I could be. I would get those needs met through my extended family. And I have! I still feel some pangs about not having children, but I had tons of time with my nieces and nephews while they were growing up, and that was a blessing. They all lived pretty close by, so I could always get my "baby fix."

VEDA: My parents divorced when I was six years old. Since I was the oldest, I took care of my younger siblings. I was responsible for them for so many years that I didn't have much fun as a teenager. I was busy cooking and being the mom. By the time I met Kathy, I had already spent a lot of years raising children.

KATHY: When my brother died of a drug overdose, he left behind three children under the age of five. They were taken away from their mother, who was unable to care for them at that time, and split up by Child Protective Services. The two boys were sent to foster homes. We became coguardians, with my mom, of our niece, Chrissy.

VEDA: We moved in order to be closer to Kathy's mother and jointly care for Chrissy. We became instant parents, and it was a difficult transition for all of us. She was used to living in difficult circumstances, and expected us to beat her when she acted out, but we never did. Chrissy lived with us for a year when she was in middle school.

Great losses can generate great compassion

KATHY: A couple of years after my younger brother died, my older brother, who had been diagnosed with paranoid schizophrenia, committed suicide. Veda and I had been together for a few years at this point. I was in a deep funk for a long time, but she was right there with me and never tried to rush me through the process. She let me grieve my two brothers' deaths, which had occurred so close together. I think one of the things that has strengthened our relationship has been her compassion and patience with me.

VEDA: I didn't really understand what Kathy was going through at the time because I had never lost a young relative. But then when my sister died, I realized, "This is really hard. Now I know what Kathy went through."

I think we have been good role models for all our nieces and nephews. Our niece Chrissy had a hard time for a while, but she's doing great now. And her two brothers are also doing well. We were able to hang in there long enough for things to come full circle.

KATHY: We've had to go through a lot of trials dealing with each other's families. Veda sets good boundaries, and she's helped me establish my own boundaries with my family and others. I never have to worry that Veda feels like a martyr or that she's being asked to give too much. She knows how to take good care of herself, and I've learned from her to do the same.

VEDA: Although we have a lot in common, we have different personalities and very different points of view. But we've learned to deal with our differences by talking things through and really listening to each other. We're both committed to having a respectful relationship, and that mutual intention has helped us learn to handle our differences in ways that were not often demonstrated in our homes when we were children.

We don't argue, but we do have passionate discussions. Respect is the key word. Our attitude is that we are just going to work it out. Sometimes I may have to stretch a little, but I never compromise my integrity. Neither of us does. We are not becoming more like each other, but rather more uniquely ourselves. At times we've hurt each other by being rude or inconsiderate, and each of those episodes is a black mark on my heart. I don't want to add any more black marks.

KATHY: We can't be legally married, but in every other sense we feel married. A spirit of goodwill characterizes our relationship. We are each careful not to martyr ourselves — we support one another but know where to draw the line so as to not overgive. We've both cultivated a lot of patience. When I was sick and in the hospital, Veda stayed in my hospital room and slept on a cot. She brought her laptop computer to continue working and didn't leave my side. I know her presence helped me heal more quickly.

VEDA: We take good care of our relationship each and every day. We kiss each other good-bye whenever we part, and we kiss each other hello whenever we reunite. We never miss kissing goodnight before we go to bed, and Kathy often gently rests her hand on my hip or back as we drift off to sleep. There is never a question in our minds that we are there for each other. The difficulties that life has offered up have just brought us closer.

Kathy has awakened me to many different kinds of experiences that I otherwise would not have had. But we also both know that we need to honor our own styles and not make sacrifices that leave us feeling neglected or resentful. It can be a tricky balance, but I think we're both doing a great job of taking care of each other and ourselves.

We're committed to living in gratitude for what we have. We feel so blessed to have a lovely home, a beautiful yard, kind neighbors, and a church full of people who, though they are not blood relatives, we experience as family.

KATHY: In most ways, our lives are very ordinary. Neither of us drinks or does drugs. We're into sports and healthy mainstream activities. We live, for the most part, almost boringly conventional lives, and our church is a foundational part — the congregation is our extended family.

VEDA: Before we became involved with our church a few years ago, we were both vaguely aware of a longing for something beyond the daily routine. We knew this was not all there was to life, but we weren't certain what else there was or where to find it. I often felt tired and saddened by all the responsibilities I was carrying in my life. I frequently felt it was up to me to keep all the plates spinning, but when we became involved with our spiritual community I stopped feeling so alone, as if an enormous weight had been lifted. Also, whereas my work used to be practically my whole life outside of our relationship, now it's just another part of my life.

We recently had our twenty-fifth anniversary party at our church. One hundred and eight people showed up. All the family members and friends we invited came to our party, and it was the most ecstatic party we've ever had. We've had gatherings that included a lot of family members, but they haven't always been happy occasions. Sometimes we've gathered for a funeral or because someone is sick, but this was a joyful event, and it was clear that everyone there was really happy, and happy for us!

KATHY: So my bottom line is: surround yourself with people who embody love, respect, compassion, character, and courage. We find those qualities in each other and in our friends. One of my favorite quotes is "The greatest thing you'll ever learn is just to love and be loved in return" [Eden Ahbez].

VEDA: For me, it is knowing my truth, following my heart, and being persistent. I knew from the beginning that I wanted to share my life with Kathy, and that I would do whatever was necessary to make it happen. And I did, and it has been all that I hoped it would be and more, much more.

[Kathy and Veda were legally married on August 2, 2008.]

16.

GREAT MARRIAGES REQUIRE BOTH PARTNERS TO BE TEACHERS AND STUDENTS

Jack Lee Rosenberg and Beverly Kitaen Morse

J ack and Beverly became a couple in 1985, and they married ten
years later. Unbeknownst to either of them, their paths had crossed
decades earlier when they were children growing up in the same neighborhood in San Diego and attending the same schools. They never
knew of each other until they were both well into their forties and had
moved to Los Angeles. A number of synchronistic events had occurred
in their lives over the years, as though foreshadowing a future in which
they were meant to be together.

Trained as psychotherapists, Jack and Beverly are codirectors of
the Integrative Body Psychotherapy Institute. They have authored several books and have led seminars and trained mental health professionals throughout the world. Committed to living their teachings in
their marriage, they maintain a high standard of integrity.

Using their marriage as a curriculum for growth and awakening,
Jack and Beverly developed a system for professionals who work with
couples and published it in their book *The Intimate Couple*. While their
current work together appears effortless and seamless, it hasn't always
been so. Jack was much more experienced as a teacher and group leader
than Beverly when they first began working together, and the gap in
their levels of expertise activated some valuable, but at times difficult,
learning opportunities for them both. Working with these differences
forced them to cultivate aspects of themselves that otherwise might not
have been developed.

In 1996, just as it seemed they had their biggest challenges behind them, Jack was diagnosed with a life-threatening condition that required immediate open-heart surgery. Complications from the surgery resulted in the long-term impairment of his functioning both personally and professionally. Jack was no longer able to manage the responsibilities he had previously carried, and Beverly had to take on the lead role in their personal and professional lives. It was like enrolling in a crash course in leadership. Suddenly on the fast track, she had to dig more deeply to find the necessary strength and wisdom to keep the institute, the seminars, and their marriage vital and healthy, or risk losing it all.

In the meanwhile, Jack had challenges of his own. Accustomed to being in charge, he suddenly found himself dependent on others to a degree he had never experienced in his adult life. The new reality that they would share for more than two years resulted in a transformation that left them more whole, better balanced, and better integrated, both as individuals and as a couple, than ever before. These gifts did not come easily.

Jack and Beverly's story reminds us that our deepest intentions frequently provide us with the kinds of life experiences that promote development of the inner qualities we need to strengthen in order to live the lives that our hearts deeply desire. It also reminds us that we must be careful of what we ask for, because we just might get it!

Through diligence, determination, and a powerful, shared commitment, Jack and Beverly not only survived this challenge but also came through it with greater strength, love, and wisdom than they had previously experienced. Like many great teachers, the two were motivated to serve by a commitment to their own personal growth and a deep desire to pass on to others the treasured lessons from their experiences.

JACK: There are some remarkable synchronicities in our lives. Although we didn't meet for the first time until we'd reached our forties, Beverly and I were born in the same town, San Diego, and in the same hospital. I was born five years before her. We grew up in houses only six blocks apart. Our homes had the same floor plan, and we slept in the corresponding bedrooms. We went to the same elementary school and junior high school, and later we each had four children with our first spouses, and each named our second child Melissa Ann. I used to be a dentist, and for a time Beverly was a dental assistant. Our fathers had stores a few blocks apart.

BEVERLY: We have always had a fantasy that we crossed each other's paths unknowingly. Jack and I met several times professionally, in our study and practice of psychotherapy, and through mutual friends. At the end of a class on sexuality that my former husband and I attended, I was asked to keep the class going by taking over leadership. I had heard of Jack's work on the subject and invited him to be one of the speakers. Later I joined Jack's organization, and it wasn't long before our professional relationship became more personal.

When Jack and I first became a couple, we were determined not to let anything dampen our love and passion. As experienced practitioners we used all our mind and body skills to sustain our own well-being and clarity. Every evening we cleared any upsets that might have existed between us. Still, we began to notice that old, destructive themes from previous relationships had begun to creep into our lives. We had made a commitment to face our own habitual relational patterns as they showed up, and, seeing the parts we were playing, we could no longer blame the other, or our former spouses, for certain past hurts.

Jack and I wanted to be as emotionally close as possible, so we did as much as we could together. We cooked, shopped, played, worked with groups and couples, led workshops, taught at and ran our institute, and wrote books together. In such close quarters we were bound to step on each other's toes. Trust became imperative. I trusted Jack and truly believed that he felt the same, and that he was not out to get me. We decided that, no matter how injured we felt at the time of an upset, we would assume a misunderstanding had occurred, and that our partner's intention was positive.

Teaching together was a challenge in the beginning. When we first started to facilitate our workshops, Jack had been a therapist for many years. He was the expert and a published author, and he had name recognition. When I joined as a teacher and workshop leader, I was relatively inexperienced, while he enjoyed a worldwide following. Initially I was intimidated. Could I sit next to him, be a partner, and let him have his brilliance, experience, skills, and bag of tricks? It took time, a lot of journal work, a leap of faith, and encouragement from Jack to keep me from diminishing myself. We both knew how important it was to have absolute equality and reciprocity in order to develop mutuality and sustain love in a relationship. Because of the nature of our work, we had to learn to carry the load equally, otherwise the group would not respect us or our work.

JACK: I remember one day saying to Beverly, "Don't lie down. Own what you know as a human being. Don't giggle after you say something profound; it discounts you and what you have just said."

BEVERLY: At first I was hurt. Then I had to acknowledge to myself that Jack was right. I was purposely, although unconsciously, trying to make myself smaller in the hope of making others feel more comfortable. But I eventually rose to the challenge of finding my voice. I had to.

JACK: We never ask our students to do anything we haven't lived ourselves — it makes us tremendously uncomfortable to be even the slightest bit dishonest. And it has always been difficult for us to work with others, especially couples, if there is an unresolved problem between us. We could never do anything to hurt the bond we share. We've learned to be careful with loaded issues. For instance, I can complain about my kids, but Beverly better not. She can complain about her kids, but God forbid if I do.

Lovemaking is a physical expression of what we feel in our hearts

BEVERLY: One thing I found especially attractive about Jack was how comfortable he was with his sexuality. His desire for me was primal and unmistakable. His sexuality came with a delightful energy rather than neediness. Shortly after my divorce from my husband of twenty-seven years, my daughter went to an office party where her father and many of his employees were gathered. Expressing true concern for a recently divorced woman of fifty, one of the men there asked my daughter, "How is your mother doing?" My daughter answered with great timing: "Oh, she's doing extremely well. She's dating the man who wrote the book *Total Orgasm*, and she is just fine."

Then, ten years into our relationship, on our wedding anniversary, Jack had to have heart bypass surgery. It really put to the test the personal and relational mental health skills that we were practicing and teaching.

JACK: I was terrified when I went for my surgery, because I had two relatives who had died from overdoses of anesthesia. I had reported this fact to my doctors, but they dismissed my concern as normal anxiety about a serious operation. With the first shot the anesthesiologist gave me, my heart stopped. I was put on a heart-lung machine for an extended period of time, which caused oxygen deprivation in my brain.

BEVERLY: During Jack's surgery, I was downstairs a couple of floors below the operating theater. Jack and I were so attuned that I knew he was in a life-or-death situation even before the doctors came to inform me. Later I could sense him being cut into during the very moments when the surgery was taking place. Sitting there with family, I realized that an overextension of closeness like this was not helpful to either of us. It was too much. I couldn't allow myself to get so stressed that I couldn't be strong, present, and alert, given all that Jack was going to need. His illness challenged me to discover how to be close, supportive, and caring without abandoning myself, and to take on the almost impossible responsibility for keeping him alive. I realized I had to be grounded in my own center for both of us.

JACK: I came out of the surgery with symptoms of senility. For the next two years, I spent a lot of time meditating. I knew I had memory loss, but I was not aware that my cognitive functioning was also impaired.

Emotionally, I felt terribly insecure, and not surprisingly, our sex life was also affected.

BEVERLY: Jack hadn't been home from the hospital very long when he wanted to have sex. When he got close to orgasm, he would say good-bye to me. Sometimes he would say things like "If I die, I'll watch over you." It was a bit too intense for me to have death mixed up with our sexual experience. I was shocked to find, for the first time, that I didn't want sex with Jack. But we have a strong commitment to each other; one of the vows we made at our wedding was that we would not allow anything to get in the way of our love or sexual passion. Over time, we were able to eliminate the anxiety-provoking sexual atmosphere by keeping the death conversations separate from our sexual interaction.

Balancing a relationship is an ongoing process, not a fixed event

JACK: This crisis also changed the nature of our relationship: I had to go inward to heal, and Beverly had to turn outward to take over managing our personal and professional lives. This dramatically shifted the balance of our relationship. Having separate domains put a dent in our closeness.

BEVERLY: After Jack's heart surgery, two of the six bypass grafts broke down, and his doctor told me he might not ever fully recover. That stunned me. I felt overwhelmed. Was the rest of my life going to be confiscated by this illness? I had worked so hard to stop making the needs of others more important than my own.

As it turned out, this was not to be the case. Over the next few years, we wrote two books together, and it was a tremendous challenge to coauthor them with equal voices. But anything this difficult is an opportunity, because it forces me to learn and grow. Many people look for formulas for relationships, but formulas don't work in the long term. The only thing we've found that works over the long term is to show up in the moment and tell the truth. Only when we are honest with ourselves can we be truly intimate with someone we love.

JACK: It is imperative that I let go of anything that might threaten my relationship to myself or to Beverly. Practices that bring us closer, like breathing together and skin time, we make a priority. We spend a great deal of time doing what brings us the most enjoyment. I am committed to making sure that Beverly has the experience of knowing and feeling how much I adore her.

BEVERLY: I have always appreciated Jack's intelligence and honor and especially his ability to make intense contact with me, but what I love the most about him is that I can always trust him to take what I say into consideration. Our shared commitment to truth and authenticity is a powerful force that has given us life-changing, heartfelt moments, and I wouldn't have had it any other way!

17.

SOMETIMES YOU HAVE TO
RISK IT ALL TO HAVE IT ALL

Jane Morton and Michael Jacobs

Jane and Michael could easily be described as a "power couple." They are among the top physicians of their respective fields and have been long-term faculty members at Stanford University School of Medicine. But what makes these two unique is not simply their long list of professional achievements or even the extremely high regard in which their colleagues and community hold them. It is their ability, when faced with challenges, to mobilize the commitment necessary to successfully meet them.

Their first challenge was one that many couples in second marriages face: blending two families without diminishing the integrity of the marriage. As all too many people know from firsthand experience, having to decide whether to prioritize the children or the marriage is one of the most difficult aspects of blended families and one a disturbingly high number of couples fail to resolve.

Jane and Michael's second major challenge was another one that an increasingly high percentage of families deal with: managing job stress and burnout. What is most impressive about these two people is their willingness, when faced with the consequences of their all-consuming passion for their work, to risk it all. When confronted with the need for a major life change, they completely removed themselves from their secure, predictable, and prestigious but stressed-out life. What began as a temporary break from a deadening routine morphed into a sixteen-month pilgrimage that transformed nearly every aspect of their personal and professional lives. Theirs is a story of integrity, courage, creativity, and spontaneity. With no guarantees of what, if anything, would be waiting when they returned, they set out into the mystery.

Sometimes success itself can be the biggest obstacle to growth and change. Michael and Jane did have a lot to lose in leaving their careers and home for an indefinite period of time. But it wasn't just their need to restructure their lives that compelled them to make their move. It was a deep and overwhelming urge to experience a life of greater peace, balance, and wholeness. Their conviction that together they could fulfill their dreams has kept them on track. Theirs is truly a joint venture, one that neither could have pulled off alone, and it has brought them far more than they ever anticipated.

JANE: We've been together for twenty-seven years. We have a California family — his, mine, and ours — with a total of three kids and two grandchildren. Michael and I met at a Disaster Committee Meeting at the hospital where we are both physicians. I kept noticing him, thinking, "God, this guy is so cool." I had my eye on him throughout the meeting. We had only a brief conversation at the end of the meeting, but that was enough to launch me into a full-blown fantasy of the life we would create together. It was irrational and nutty, I know, to fall so hard with only a small amount of information about someone, but the attraction was overpowering. I loved the soft tone of his voice and was impressed with the words that came out of his mouth. A few days later, when I received a love poem signed "Michael," I went into a swoon and then memorized the entire poem. The fantasy that had been budding bloomed in full flower. I was so enchanted that I wrote a poem to him and signed it "J." When he got it, he didn't know who I was. It seems there had been a mix-up; the poem I received had come from another Michael. I had to call him up to explain what had happened. It was so embarrassing!

MICHAEL: It was clear to Jane from the start that we were meant to be together, but I was slower to discover this truth. We fell passionately in love. There was a strong sexual attraction and a great deal that we admired about each other. But this did not preclude our having difficulties. We have very different ways of dealing with tension — I get quiet; Jane likes to talk about things right away. Some of the issues were fundamental, but others were trivial and childish. For instance, if she commented on my driving, it triggered old authority issues that I have about being told what to do.

At the beginning, when our trust wasn't high, Jane thought I was punishing her with my silence. It really wasn't that; it's just that when I find myself in emotional turmoil, I feel out of control. When I take some time to soothe myself and look at what I'm feeling, I can more easily calm down. I need that time of quiet because I'm an introvert. It doesn't take me too long, though; after about twenty minutes or so, I'm usually able to reconnect and speak coherently and constructively with her.

JANE: I, on the other hand, am an extrovert. When I'm stressed, I want to talk about it right away. Michael has helped me learn to be patient and not take things personally. I used to have a hard time doing that, but caring about Michael so deeply has allowed me to trust him and give him the space he needs for himself. He comes to me at the first possible moment, because he knows I want to talk things out in order to feel complete. We have a lot of balance now in the way we work on difficult issues, and of course we've handled so many of the old issues that not many crop up these days.

MICHAEL: In the early years, our biggest challenge was our blended family. Putting our two daughters together was such an ordeal that it practically destroyed us, and it probably would have if we hadn't been absolutely committed to making it work. The challenge of the blended family has been both hugely demanding and hugely rewarding. Our daughters were five and six years old when we got married, and they were as opposite as could be. My daughter, Lauren, was an outgoing city slicker who wasn't into school at all. Jane's daughter, Emma, was shy, loved school, loved books, and was the teacher's pet. Then we had a baby together, Michael, who became the glue that connected us all. Everyone doted on him and adored him, and he just reflected our smiles back to us with his adorable face.

JANE: Lauren and Emma were salt and pepper. They were so totally different that they didn't compete with each other. Every Wednesday and every other weekend, Lauren came to be with us, and because she wasn't living with us, she often felt like an outsider. When she felt left out, she behaved in ways that made us want to leave her out, so it became a self-fulfilling prophecy. We were both working long and hard in those days, and on the weekends we were desperate to relax, but many of those weekends blew up in our faces. The blowups made us even more determined to make our blended family work no matter what.

Lauren was testing to see if she could misbehave and still be loved. Early on, when our relationship was not as strong, Michael didn't fully trust me, and when I gave Lauren boundaries, and feedback about her behavior, he would come to her defense and interfere, thinking I was being too harsh. But once our relationship got stronger and he trusted me more, he didn't butt in. He knew I cared, and was not retaliating, and he backed off and let us have our own relationship. This allowed me to be more honest with Lauren about what was acceptable and what wasn't. One time we were going on a river trip, and I told Lauren that the only way she could come with us was if she promised not to misbehave and ruin the trip. It seemed like a harsh thing to say, but she promised and kept her word.

Making your marriage the highest priority is a gift to your children

MICHAEL: From the beginning, our overriding philosophy has been that our couplehood, not the children, should be the center of our universe. We decided to let every other vacation be just for us, without the children, and we stuck to it. It's important for all couples to do this, but I believe it's even more imperative for blended families. Lauren wanted me to return to her mother so we could be one happy family under one roof. She did everything she could think of to break up my marriage to Jane in the hope that I would return to her mother. By taking a firm stand alongside Jane, I made it clear to Lauren that she was not going to break us up, period! I came to understand that the kids are better served if a couple's relationship is strong, and we both worked continually to strengthen it, but boy oh boy, was it a ton of work!

JANE: I have a wonderful relationship with both of the girls now. Both of our daughters have children of their own, and Lauren calls me regularly, asking for advice about bringing up her kids. It certainly took a long time to develop such a terrific relationship with everyone in the family, but it's been worth it! We're getting ready to all go on another family vacation, with the three generations. We know we're going to have a wonderful time.

After we got some mastery of the blended family, another huge challenge came our way. This wasn't about family; it was about work. In nearly every conceivable way, we were viewed by our family and colleagues as the ideal couple with the ideal life. There was just one thing wrong: we were both experiencing advanced burnout in our careers, complete with the typical accompanying symptoms of exhaustion, emotional and physical depletion, and depression, and were feeling overwhelmed and despairing.

MICHAEL: At the end of a typical ten-hour workday, I would drive home and sob quietly in my car before coming into the house. I was waking up at 5 AM and dragging myself home at 7 PM or later. It wasn't just the amount of work that I was doing, it was the nature of the system that I was doing it in. I got into medicine because I wanted to help people, but the medical system over the years had become increasingly dehumanized. I found myself with less and less time to spend with my patients and more and more people to see — at the time, my practice included over twenty-five hundred people. I'd come home from work exhausted by my efforts to deal with a system that was a battlefield of warring factions.

One evening after a particularly demanding day at work, I asked

Jane to sit down with me before dinner. I said to her, "I've gotten to the point where I just can't take it anymore." It was no secret to Jane that I'd become ragged around the edges. She'd known that things had been unraveling for me, and I knew that her situation wasn't much better. We'd both been just holding on, hoping or praying for something to change. That night I realized nothing was going to change unless we did something about it.

JANE: Michael and I decided to take a vacation to see if we could restore ourselves by getting off the treadmill for a while. We knew we had to leave immediately. We couldn't wait. We decided to go to New England and left within a week. We found a peaceful, romantic country inn in Vermont that provided the perfect setting for the R & R we so desperately needed. It was such a stark contrast with our lives at home.

MICHAEL: The questions that kept coming up were: What would it take to integrate this quality of peace into our lives at home? Would we have to move, or leave our jobs? Did we want to? Was doing so a real possibility or simply a fantasy? At the end of the vacation, we came home without having definitively answered all the questions, but were deeply committed to somehow doing whatever was needed to integrate the "Vermont experience" into our daily lives. Knowing it was available, we couldn't continue living the way we had been living. Weeks after returning from Vermont, we found ourselves back in the pressure cooker. We had lost all that we gained on vacation, and in some ways it was even worse because we had had a taste of life without stress.

When you gotta go, you gotta go!

JANE: One day I returned from the market with several bags of groceries. Michael came out to meet me, but he didn't offer to help carry them into the house. "Leave them," he said. "There's something more important that we need to handle. Now." I knew something big was up — Michael's never been one to be dramatic. I had a pretty good sense of what he was going to say, and I was right.

MICHAEL: "Jane," I said, "this just isn't working. We've fallen back into the same rut we were in before we went to Vermont. But now it feels even more unbearable. I can't take it anymore — I'm burnt to a crisp. Something's got to give, and it's going to have to be more than another three-week vacation. We need a major overhaul. This is our opportunity to make the life change we've been talking about — I mean, really do it, not just talk about what we would like to do. If we don't take the leap now, when will we? Why don't we each tell our bosses that we want to, that we need to take a leave of absence?"

JANE: I asked Michael, "For how long?" And Michael told me, "I don't know... indefinitely, or as long as it takes to bring balance into our lives and have some peace and sanity, not just temporarily, but permanently." I was scared at the prospect of proposing this to the director of my program. I couldn't imagine this person consenting to an indefinite leave of absence, but at the same time I couldn't imagine continuing the way we were, either. I quickly went from feeling scared about Mike's proposal to being incredibly excited, like a kid anticipating an adventure. By the end of the evening, we had agreed to do it, to take a huge chunk of time off, at least a year, and give ourselves permission to live off the grid, off the schedule, off the clock that had enslaved us for so many years. We would do what we felt inclined to do and go where we felt drawn to go. I was so excited that night, anticipating the freedom we would have, that I couldn't sleep. Oh, and Michael did eventually help bring in the groceries, but of course by then the ice cream had melted.

MICHAEL: Both of us got permission for modified leaves of absence from our jobs, although not without some resistance from the administrative higher-ups, who were reluctant to grant open-ended leaves. They were afraid we might never come back to work, which was of course a real possibility. But Jane and I were absolutely clear that if they didn't give us the time off, we would leave anyway, so I guess they felt they didn't have a choice.

JANE: We got a renter for our home and sold most of the furniture. At this point, all the kids were grown and on their own. Within two weeks we were ready to hit the road. We left with nothing but a few clothes and our three dogs in the car. The only rule we had was that we wouldn't make any plans more than twenty-four hours in advance. We were totally open to taking whatever paths we felt drawn to. It was thrilling.

MICHAEL: It took us two weeks to get to Portland, Oregon, and we realized that, at this rate, it would take about four years to get to New England — if we ever turned right. [Laughs.]

JANE: The trip turned out to be an absolutely to-die-for experience. For the first time in our lives, we had a chance to stand outside the fishbowl and look in. Opportunities and possibilities came up that we never could have taken advantage of when we were working.

MICHAEL: For me, the trip involved a lot of deep soul reflection about things that were really important to me, but that I had previously been way too busy to think about. I wanted to be free and to feel awed by life again, the way I had when I was younger. I knew it was possible to re-experience that. The more distance, literally and figuratively, that we put between ourselves and our old life, the more certain I became that I wanted something else. We brought *some* aspects of our former life with us, practices that we both really value. We're both runners, and we continued to exercise every day. I maintained a long-distance phone relationship with my therapist that was enormously helpful. In addition, we took on some life-enriching new activities, including yoga and meditation, and painting for Jane.

JANE: Before the trip, we were both slaves to the clock. I think I looked at my wristwatch a hundred times a day. On the trip, Michael would wake up first, and he would feed the dogs and spend some time reading, and I would gradually wake up. It was such a luxury to take as much time as we wanted to do whatever we felt like doing, which often was nothing. We tried new things we hadn't done — I really got into art and painting, and did some cross-country skiing. The whole period was a time of reflection for us both. All of the time and energy that had been spent in service to others was now for us to use for us. It was so luxurious! I loved waking slowly each day, on my body's timetable, rather than in reaction to the shrill ring of an alarm clock.

MICHAEL: We returned home after sixteen months on the road, but the transition back home was not easy and proved to be unsettling for both of us.

JANE: We were concerned about losing the experience of freedom that we'd felt while we were gone, and afraid of falling into some of the same old patterns. We checked in with our friends frequently to make sure we weren't backsliding. Our process didn't stop; we continued to take stock of our lives and had to keep reminding ourselves that we were here to take care of each other and not the whole world.

MICHAEL: We continued to make changes designed to integrate the experience on the road into our ongoing lives. Shortly after returning, we did leave our jobs and assumed new professional positions that were less consuming but equally fulfilling. Before we'd gone on our trip, I'd had such a large patient load that I was able to spend fifteen minutes at most with each patient. Shortly after we returned, I left the position I had at Stanford and started up a retainer practice with less than one-tenth the number of patients I'd had, about 250. That allowed me the luxury of spending an hour and a half or more with patients. I could really connect with them. Five to ten percent of the people I see in my current practice are low-income and pay me nothing for my services. My experience of practicing medicine has entirely transformed as a result of this change.

JANE: I still paint and have produced a number of pieces in watercolor and acrylics. We've both continued a lot of what we began on the road. Michael meditates at least five times a week. The clock no longer runs us, and neither of us sees patients before 10 AM. We both love having the luxury of spending more time with individual patients than we could in our former positions. We are home by 5 PM every day, and we still don't use an alarm clock.

Self-care is an act of generosity

MICHAEL: One of the most important things I learned on that road trip is that you can't give more to someone else than you give to yourself. By learning how to take good care of myself on our trip, I now have much more to give Jane and the other people in my life. It clearly has been a transformative experience for me. We could never return to the pressure-cooker life we lived for so many years. We've come too far and seen too much to ever go there again. We cherish the ease and peace that we now live with every day, which allows us all kinds of pleasures that we didn't have time for, including sex.

JANE: Sexuality has always been a strong part of our relationship. We've had powerful sexual chemistry from the very beginning, and it has gotten even stronger over time. It has helped us through some difficult times. I've always known that a good sexual connection was absolutely necessary for me. Several years into our marriage, I had a hysterectomy, and for the first time in life, with my uterus and ovaries gone, I started to have sexual problems.

My desire was way down, and I was pretty unresponsive to stimulation that I had previously found delightful. I was in a state of grief and despair, fearing that sexual pleasure was only a part of my past. I was deeply frustrated and unhappy. But Michael was great. He was patient and steady. He had a wonderful attitude that helped us become more relaxed, playful, and experimental. We created a whole new repertory of practices that we hadn't been motivated to cultivate before, when I had all my hormones. It has involved a lot of trust, communication, and creativity, but it has really paid off.

MICHAEL: We believe that the great pleasure we derive from our sexual connection is an important part of keeping our life in balance. There is no way we could be as productive, and have a good attitude, without that special energy between us. It is a powerful way that we connect and get ready to go out on the front lines again to make our contributions.

JANE: Without Michael's support, I couldn't possibly have done professionally what I've done. But the support hasn't come only from

Michael. It's come from our friends who have been there with us and for us throughout all our challenges, both personal and professional. We don't have a lot of friends, but the ones we do, know us inside and out and have been with us for years. We really need them, and vice versa. We're all truly there for each other. I can't emphasize enough just how valuable these relationships have been to us.

And the more we grow, the more we have to give each other and others. As valuable and necessary as our connections with our friends are, Michael is still my number one supporter. He's always there to remind me in ways that no one else can that I'm capable and intelligent. He helps me keep my sense of humor. When I feel like I'm swimming in molasses, wondering if I'm getting anywhere, he reminds me how far we've come. When there are factions vying to dominate turf at work, he helps me stay calm and see the big picture. Michael has prompted so much of my personal and professional growth.

Great marriages can be as healing as the best therapy

JANE: What I have experienced in this marriage is better than the best therapy in the world! I am literally not the same person I was when I met Michael, and neither is he. We both had reservations when we were first together, fearing that the relationship would not pass the test of time and still be vibrant twenty-five years later. That has not turned out to be the case. If anything, our passion and love for each other has grown, not diminished. I live with the certainty that I love Michael more today than I did yesterday, and that I will love him more tomorrow than I do today. Of all the achievements of my life, and there have been many, the greatest is what we have created together. It's the one that brings me the most joy.

18.

THE THREE SECRETS TO SUCCESS IN MARRIAGE ARE COMMITMENT, COMMITMENT, AND COMMITMENT

Ken and Maddy Dychtwald

Ken Dychtwald has come a long way from his New Jersey roots. His expansive office on the thirty-sixth floor, overlooking the San Francisco Bay, is filled with awards and photographs of him with celebrities, presidents, and other world leaders. Generally recognized as a leading authority on aging and gerontology, Ken has done an enormous amount to help the public see older age not as a time of decline and deterioration but as one of ripening into one's fullest potential, where life is characterized by continued purpose-filled contribution and growth.

After studying, researching, and writing about the phenomenon of older age for more than three decades, Ken and his wife, Maddy, are themselves entering this stage of life. While much of Ken's expertise has been based on theory, these days life experience grounds this couple in the principles of what they call "conscious aging."

Ken and Maddy embody these principles in their daily lives, living with a spirit of passionate aliveness, ongoing gratitude, and a shared dedication to service. Yet Ken's greatest accomplishment, the one he is most proud of, is not related to his work. It is the marriage and family he and Maddy have created together. A public speaker and an award-winning author, Maddy is every bit a match for her dynamic husband. Throughout their twenty-five years of marriage, she has been both the recipient of his love, support, and guidance and a tremendous source of support and validation for those qualities in him.

The couple's marriage is based on equality, reciprocity, and mutual respect, all of which were evident to us throughout our interview, as was their humor and playfulness. Their comfort in relating to each other and to us reflected the inner peace and self-acceptance that Ken and Maddy experience and reinforce in each other. Like athletes who are in the "zone," or artists in the flow, these two ride the current of life with grace and ease. It's no wonder they inspire so many.

KEN: When Maddy and I met, I was thirty-one and she was twenty-nine. I had never been married. I was single and having a complete blast, gliding around from one relationship to another, thinking, "The single life is fantastic." To me, marriage seemed like San Quentin State Prison. I wasn't looking for a long-term relationship, and neither was Maddy. A mutual friend thought we might hit it off and gave me Maddy's phone number.

MADDY: I had been married before. I got married at twenty-one and was much too immature for it to work out. My first husband and I were both spoiled, both used to getting what we wanted. When I left that marriage, I had a huge realization: "Marriage isn't something I have to have in my life to be happy." I was gun-shy about going after the life-partner model and comfortable with a series of three-year relationships. Whenever a partner wanted to take it to a deeper level, I broke it off every time. I was in a relationship when Ken and I met.

KEN: In our first phone conversation, we discovered that we grew up just a few miles from one another in New Jersey. We went to different high schools and had never met. We got into having regular phone conversations every night, and we sent each other our press kits. We spoke on the phone every day for six months before we met in person.

MADDY: When Ken told me he was a psychologist, our friendship really deepened. I began to open up to him about my inner life. He sent me a copy of the book *Bodymind*, which he had written when he was only twenty-three. In the book, he shared some intimate details of his life. The relationship I was in at the time was beginning to deteriorate, and so I decided it was once again time to leave. Ken suggested that we meet in person, and I agreed.

KEN: I remember being at the airport, waiting for her flight at the gate, then watching the passengers coming through. I felt my heart beating in my chest. I was thirty-one years old, but I felt like a teenager on his first date. When I saw Maddy, I was overwhelmed with excitement and love, as though I'd known her my whole life — it felt like a reunion, not a meeting. The first night we were together, we had a discussion about our deepest fears in relationship. We got right down to it immediately.

MADDY: For me, it was definitely love at first sight. By the next day, I was certain I wanted to be with Ken forever.

KEN: Up to this point, I'd had little tolerance for being with anyone; all of my prior relationships had been brief. My style had been to get into a relationship and tire of it quickly. But this time there was something different going on; Maddy was interesting and powerful. We were living in separate towns, and when she left I missed her terribly. I was surprised at what I was feeling, because I had never missed a woman before.

MADDY: Not long after our relationship began to intensify, I got into a motorcycle accident and broke my nose and some other bones in my face. This interfered with my career as an actress in soap operas in Los Angeles. I walked away from my work and moved in with Ken, where I spent the next year healing from the accident.

KEN: I was happy for her to move in. Maddy was different from anyone I had ever been with. She had so much more fire than the other women. I was attracted to the energy that matched my own fire, but we had to learn how to manage it so it didn't burn us both to a crisp. I remember one time early in our relationship when we were arguing, and Maddy stood up to me and said, "It's obvious that you have a list of requirements that you are looking for in a woman. I'm not that person, but if you put aside your list long enough to check me out, you will find that I'm much better for you than what you have on your list." She was right.

When two people share an intention, everything changes

MADDY: We were madly in love with each other, but we were still both commitment-phobic. One night, Ken sat down and drew a circle and said, "This is a circle of commitment. Are we inside or outside? If we're outside, there isn't much at stake, and not much is possible. If we're inside the circle, we're going to see each issue through until we find some place to stand together." At that moment, I had the realization, "That's what marriage is really about."

KEN: I wasn't willing to spend time fighting unless there was a commitment. In the midst of having this argument, we took a side path to discover whether we were both inside the circle of commitment while having this argument, or outside of it. It was a pivotal moment. We both realized that we were in it for the long haul, and that made all the difference when our issues came up.

MADDY: Once we committed to our relationship, things really took off. We both knew this was it. We started looking more directly into ourselves and our relationship to assess how things were going, what was problematical, and how we could improve things.

KEN: We committed ourselves to giving our relationship the highest possible care and to making whatever corrections we felt were needed. We have kept that commitment to this day and will continue to for the rest of our lives. We don't ever take our relationship for granted. Once we passed over that big threshold, marriage was the next natural step. Our wedding was so glorious that, at one point, I turned to Maddy and said, "This is wonderful; let's do it every year." Maddy said, "Okay, let's do it." And we have.

MADDY: We have a tradition of taking a week for a honeymoon each Thanksgiving. One year, we didn't take our normal week away, and it was the tensest time we've ever had. That year, we learned a big lesson: nothing comes before the well-being of our marriage. We have to continually light the fire. We get married again every year on or near our wedding anniversary — we've had twenty-five weddings so far. One year Ken rented an Elvis suit from a costume shop and we got married in the Chapel of Love in Las Vegas. We've gotten married by the singing rabbis of Marin County, and we've gotten married on a deserted tropical island, with our kids performing the ceremony. Sometimes we make elaborate plans, and sometimes the day before, we put the ceremony together. One year we were having a huge fight; we put the fight aside, had the ceremony, and picked up the fight where we left off. It's not just about the ritual of getting married; the important part is the assessment that goes on before and after the recommitment ceremony. We assess how we did during the previous year, and sculpt our marriage to fit our changing needs and goals.

KEN: This course correction is as important as anything else we do all year. In recent years, we haven't needed many major changes. When we connect on our anniversary, we always get back on track. It has become increasingly clear, with maturity, that if I push too hard on anything, it will come back to bite me on the ass. If I try to boss Maddy at work, I'll have to pay at home. When we were younger, I was concerned about holding on to my power. I didn't want her to run over me.

I've learned that I need to do everything I can to make sure Maddy is happy, so that I can be happy. When she was writing her book, I was afraid she would become famous and I might lose her. I had to choose whether I was going to hold her down in order not to lose her, or take a leap of faith. It was a huge deal for me. I realized that the only decent thing to do was to support Maddy in being the greatest person she could possibly be.

One of the biggest challenges we have had to face in our marriage is my jealousy of my own children. Parenting was a strain on us when the children were very small, and then again when they were teenagers. Now our son, Zak, and our daughter, Casey, are the lights of my life.

But I admit that I like a lot of attention, and years ago there was a certain chill that came over our marriage when I felt neglected. Maddy has always been devoted to the kids. Whenever I felt she had made the children her priority, and that the marriage had dropped in priority, I would get angry. We would find ourselves bickering and sniping. Thank God, we don't do that any more, but there were years when this was a big problem. We had to go to marriage counseling, where we got the good advice to plan more dates together.

Every relationship requires "time in the pool"

MADDY: When we went away alone together, it always helped a lot. But as soon as we neglected the husband-wife part of our system, we would feel the distress right away. Everyone I know who takes his or her relationship for granted has a poor relationship. In our case, we both travel a lot for work. We were traveling alone and alternating our trips so that the children would have one of us at home. During an annual marriage assessment, we realized that that was great for the children, but not for our relationship. We decided to spend time together at least once a month, hiking and walking and talking together, really communicating. We sandwich a day together between business trips, even when it's inconvenient. These plans often take us out of our way, but we take days off from work to take care of our relationship. We've come to refer to it as "time in the pool." When we were teaching the children to swim, they became great swimmers because we got into the pool with them and spent a lot of time there assisting them in perfecting their swimming skills. Similarly, we've spent a great deal of time perfecting our relationship skills, and the requirements have changed over the years.

KEN: Things were very different during our first few years together. We didn't have any money. Early in our marriage Maddy and I started a company together, and we have worked together ever since. I became intrigued by business and fell in love with the juice of the game. At one point, I raised a hundred million dollars. The company was becoming more and more successful, beyond what I ever imagined. We had over a thousand people working for us in twelve states. I was on the cover of national magazines. We began to think of ourselves as Bill and Melinda Gates. Then when I was fifty, the business venture cratered — one by one, like a house of cards, each segment of the business fell. I felt like an utter failure; I had never experienced depression before. We lost our money and our savings. I was beyond broken — I felt utterly destroyed. The worst part was that I didn't know if I would ever get out of it. It was a very bad year.

No matter what you lose, if you still have a solid marriage you have everything

MADDY: The loss of the business wasn't worrisome to me — I was optimistic about our future. We had young kids at the time. They were happy, we had a good marriage, and I was convinced we could just begin again.

KEN: Maddy tried to reassure me, but I couldn't sleep because I was having such bad nightmares. I was embarrassed to go outside to see people, and profoundly ashamed of myself. A therapist I saw was helpful when he said, "Don't be in too much of a hurry to get out of this place you're in. It will make you a better person." I began to see that I had been so caught up in my ambitions that I hadn't been fully present with the people in my life, even those I loved most. I examined some of my assumptions about what success is, and realized I had been defining success from the outside, not the inside. I was buying into ideas that had been handed to me, without finding out what success really meant to me personally.

My brother said just the right thing when I was open to hearing it. He asked if Maddy and I were doing all right. I told him that we were fine together and the marriage was strong. He asked how the children were, and I told him the children were healthy and happy. My brother said, "Then you have everything." I let that message penetrate me, and that's the moment when I started to get my spirit back. Nowadays, I do only those parts of the business that I really enjoy. I love writing and speaking engagements, but sitting on business boards is boring. And as fate would have it, the business is thriving again now, and I am enjoying it more than ever.

In my life, I've had all kinds of advantages, financially and educationally, but the primary driving force in my success is Maddy. She believes in me so much that I feel I can do whatever I set my mind to. I am constantly working with elderly people, who are at the end of their lives and looking back on the choices they made. I hear much too much "I wish I had . . ." (fill in the blank). I don't want to get to the end of my life, look back, and have any "I wish I had's." I don't want to ever look back on my life with regret.

MADDY: When I first met Ken, I was struck by his good looks, his intelligence, and his sense of humor, and over time I came to see his flaws as well. Instead of focusing on them, I choose to focus on his qualities that I love and his abilities, which are continually growing and developing. He has inspired me to push myself beyond my limits. He's helped me find my voice and realize my personal power. This is so far beyond what I ever expected from a spouse. "It's okay if you fail," Ken told me. "Just give it your best shot." He helped me see that the only real failure lies in not trying. Ken has been like a proud parent regarding my accomplishments, and sometimes I get a little embarrassed by his pride in me, but mostly it makes me happy, happier than I ever imagined I could be.

19.

NOT ALL GREAT MARRIAGES
REQUIRE HARD WORK

Hope and Laurence Juber

L aurence Juber was a nine-year-old boy in London when he first
heard the Beatles. He had no idea how his life would be affected
by that moment. Possessed by a nearly unquenchable desire to be immersed in music, which was only intensified by the sudden explosion
of Beatlemania, he hounded his parents to buy him a guitar. After two
years of begging and pleading, Laurence was given his first guitar. He
was a quick study, and by the time he was thirteen he was playing local
gigs on weekends. By age fifteen, he was performing with headliners in
the London club scene. When Laurence was twenty-four, he realized
a dream bigger than anything he had dared to hope for: he was invited
to play lead guitar for Paul McCartney in the band Wings. One might
think such an achievement would overshadow anything else he might
experience, but the best was yet to come.

Hope Juber grew up in a Hollywood family. Her father, an established writer known for his stints as head writer for Bob Hope and Red
Skelton, also created iconic TV shows such as *Gilligan's Island* and *The
Brady Bunch*. Hope played Greg Brady's girlfriend in a few episodes of
the seventies classic. And like the man she would eventually marry, she
was passionate about the Beatles. The compatibility between Hope and
Laurence goes far beyond their common love of Beatles music, however. One of the remarkable things about this enormously talented and
creative couple is that, through their marriage, they have helped each

other reach greater levels of creativity and artistry by being each other's most devoted and admiring supporter.

Both now in their fifties, Hope and Laurence display the exuberance and vitality of children. Their relationship is characterized by a playful quality that they bring to all their activities, and which was evident in our interview. Partners, lovers, parents, and cocreators, they are also playmates whose curiosity, wonder, and fascination is contagious. Even the best marriages have their difficult times, and when such moments do on occasion arise for Hope and Laurence, that's all they are — moments. Being right is less important to either than being happy, and in letting go of the need to be right, there's nothing lost and much gained. Very much.

When you're possessed by something, there's no escape

HOPE: I can't tell you about how Laurence and I met without talking about our connection to the Beatles. In a very real sense, the Beatles brought us together. I was twenty-five years old and Laurence was twenty-eight when we met. The Beatles were the source of our initial connection and in many ways have continued to be a connection for us throughout the twenty-five years we've been together. I was seven when I first heard their music, and it changed everything. They were the only thing I knew for certain could make me feel better any time. In college I even wrote a play composed entirely of Beatle lyrics. I was always the girl who loved the Beatles.

In 1980, when John was assassinated, I went into a profound depression, far worse than any before or since. The event shook my whole world. I felt like the ground beneath my feet had been ripped away. The one thing I had always relied on to make me feel better, the music of the Beatles, now caused so much pain. I couldn't believe that someone would kill, actually assassinate, an artist. I stopped eating, spent most of my time in bed, and just couldn't get over it. My parents were worried sick, and my mother kept desperately trying to think of anything that could get me out of bed and reengaged with life. She got me an appointment with her Beverly Hills hairdresser — she thought getting my hair done would make me feel better. To be honest, I thought it was pretty pointless. I couldn't have cared less about my hair at that time, but I didn't have the strength to argue, so I went along with her plan.

I dragged myself out of bed to keep the appointment. The hairdresser and I struck up a conversation, and I accepted his offer to get a bite to eat when he finished with his last client. While I was waiting for him, I went outside to walk around the block. I was so distracted that I wasn't watching, and I bumped into a person. When I looked up, I was staring into the eyes of Ringo Starr. He was with his wife, Barbara. For a moment, I was in shock and speechless, and then I apologized for stepping on him and said something about how sorry I was about John's death. I was ready to walk away, but Ringo asked if he could talk to me for a minute. I was so surprised — I had never met him or any of the Beatles before. He spoke about John's death and told me about an album he was currently working on. He spoke of work as being important to focus on, something that could help him heal. It turned out that Laurence was to play guitar on the album.

I went home and thought long and hard about what he said. Not long afterward, my dad called and asked if I would like to work on a new sitcom he was putting together. He had asked me to work for him a couple of times before, and I usually said no. I hadn't wanted to get a job, and I was going to refuse again, but then I thought for a moment and said to myself, "An opportunity to work. Maybe that's what I need. Maybe that's what the whole Ringo thing was about." And I said, "Yes, okay, I'll work on the show."

While visiting New York with a friend from work, we made plans to meet in a club. When I walked in, I overheard someone say Paul McCartney's guitar player was there. I didn't know the members of Wings, but I thought that was pretty cool. Just then three guys walked toward us, but I saw only Laurence. The connection was instantaneous and amazing. I didn't realize he was the guitarist I had heard about until much later. It sometimes feels as though it was all arranged. The whole sequence of events, meeting Ringo on the street, his message that got me back to work, flying to New York: it all seemed orchestrated. I went home with Laurence that night, and we've been together ever since.

There is much to be learned from great lovers

LAURENCE: My father, who had bought me my first guitar for my eleventh birthday, died suddenly of a heart attack at the age of fifty-one. One month later, Paul McCartney invited me to join Wings, and I felt the presence of my father's spirit with me. Paul was a creative authority figure who was significant in my life and served as a mentor. During the years I was with Wings, I was around Paul and Linda a lot and got to see what a strong and faithful marriage looked like — I spent a lot of time at their farm in Scotland. Working with Paul was much more than a career opportunity; it was a life-changing event. Knowing him and his values, and the kind of partnership he had with Linda, opened up my heart and mind to the kind of relationship I wanted.

I continued to develop my creativity and went deeper into my spiritual practice. I was feeling the last layers of the onion peeling away. One day, I felt something deep and powerful move within me, like I was experiencing a quantum leap in the process of my own awakening. I knew something special was going to happen. That was the night I met Hope. Instantly I recognized that this was the time, this was the place, this was the right woman! I told Hope on the night we met that I wanted to marry her. There never was and never has been a moment's doubt.

HOPE: I was very attracted to Laurence, and he was absolutely clear that I was the one, but I wasn't quite ready to give up the pleasures of the single life. Laurence's intense focus took me by surprise. I felt as if a big hand had come down from the sky and plucked me up and put me down where I was supposed to be. I decided to stay an extra week in New York. When I called home to say that I was extending my stay, my mom mentioned this to my father, who was standing nearby. "She's going to marry him," he said. My mother said, "Hope didn't say anything about staying in New York for a man," and my father replied, "If she's staying in New York another week, there's a man, and she's going to marry him."

Although I have no formal training in meditation, I have always been aware of the prophetic aspects of my dreams. Every morning, I tell Laurence the intricate dreams that visit me in the night, which sometimes are so vivid and elaborate that I go on for a full hour. We also have another ritual where we connect with each other when we walk our dogs, which we do twice a day. The morning ritual and the dog-walking routines free up our minds and spirits and rejuvenate us. Our daily rituals activate the creative artist and visionary in each of us. Some of our best work over the last twenty years has come out of them. It's a seamless process, where we flow from concerns about our kids to the next creative project we are dreaming up to more mundane concerns. We never run out of subjects to discuss. The projects we work on are all ours together. Our ideas feed into each other's. This process is part of our consciously being a couple. We each bring our distinct, unique point of view and our own unique gifts.

LAURENCE: We are committed to our couplehood. When we travel, we often travel together. This "couple consciousness" was formulated early in the relationship. The decisions we make sometimes look as if they're slanted toward one of us. We find, though, that when we make decisions with the well-being of the couple in mind, it works out in the long run. We've each had our turns being in the spotlight. Hope put together a rock and roll band called the Housewives, and I backed her up on guitar. In recent years, I've been out front performing. Hope has been producing my shows and doing a hell of a good job too.

HOPE: My parents were a lot like the happy couple on *The Brady Bunch*. They recently celebrated their sixty-fifth wedding anniversary, and in all those years I never saw them fight. It sounds strange, but I felt almost disadvantaged not to see any conflict in my family. When I went out into the real world, if anyone fought with me or got angry at me, it really threw me. I didn't know what to do or say.

I found that the very same thing was happening in our family. When our two daughters were younger, I realized they had not been exposed to angry situations, and I became concerned that they might not learn how to handle differences. I talked to Laurence about this, and we agreed that the kids needed to witness us being angry and making up. So we decided to stage a fight in order to convey the message to the kids that it's okay to fight, and to give an example of what a good fight could look like. The girls were five and eight years old when we tried this experiment. Funny, but I don't think they bought it at all. That was about fifteen years ago, and we haven't had one since, staged or otherwise.

LAURENCE: We do have differences and disagreements, but we handle the impulse to become angry so quickly that a dispute never comes to much. If I catch myself thinking only of my own needs, rather than the well-being of us as a couple, I check myself out. I know full well that I'm in trouble when I start thinking me, me, me. And it's just as dangerous to slip into thinking you, you, you. The kind of thinking that keeps us on the path is us, us, us.

HOPE: I have a good example of learning to make decisions that serve us both. The first time we visited England as a couple, I was excited about meeting Laurence's side of the family. We had come over from California, and Laurence's mom prepared to host a big dinner party, roasting chickens; inviting aunts, uncles, and cousins; and planning a celebration in our honor.

On the day before the festivities, Laurence's brother offered to take care of our two-year-old daughter so we could go out to dinner and have a romantic evening together. The next day, when my mother-in-law heard we had gone out to dinner without her, she threw a tantrum. She ranted and raved over the telephone, calling me selfish and inconsiderate for not inviting her to join us. She concluded her tirade by announcing that she had cancelled the celebration in my honor and thrown the chickens in the garbage, and then she slammed down the phone. Laurence told me his mom had been difficult during his childhood, but that this behavior was extreme and uncharacteristic, even for her.

I remember crying as I lay on the bed trying to figure it all out. The whole episode had taken me completely by surprise. Young and eager to please my mother-in-law and get to know Laurence's entire family, I felt misunderstood, hurt, and violated by the attack. Laurence, to his great credit, was incredibly supportive, saying, "My mother is way out of line here. I wouldn't blame you if you never want anything to do with her ever again." I was so relieved to feel understood and validated by my husband that I calmed down and began to think the situation through. I told Laurence, "You only have one mother. It's not acceptable to me to let this come between me and her or you and her. It's just not right."

Even if you're right, it's not necessary to announce it

HOPE: I called my mother-in-law and apologized to her, saying, "I was completely thoughtless to go out to dinner with Laurence and not invite you to come along. We don't see you often enough, and I want to spend time with you when we come to visit. I hope you can forgive me and come to dinner with us tonight." My mother-in-law accepted my apology, and we repaired our damaged relationship.

LAURENCE: It wasn't too long after this emotional explosion that my mom began her bouts of pneumonia, with episodes of being in and out of the hospital. She was not properly diagnosed at first, because she didn't fall into any risk category. But then it was established that she had AIDS. We never found out how she contracted it. She moved into our home, and Hope became her primary caregiver until her death. As her illness took its course, we learned that one complication of AIDS is dementia, and the previous, terrible breakdown had been the first in the series of irrational outbursts resulting from the illness's impact on her brain functioning.

I so admire Hope for being big enough to set aside issues of fairness. She had a larger vision of loving, cooperative relationships all around — herself and my mom, and herself and me. And she wanted to do what she could to preserve the tie I had with my mother. Even though Hope was young at the time, she was wise and generous. She took all responsibility for the breakdown and set my mom's mind and heart at ease. I've always felt that Hope is wise beyond her years, and this is just one of many examples I could give.

We've had very little struggle in our relationship in all these years we've been together, but that doesn't mean we haven't had hardship. A few years ago our oldest daughter, Nico, was off at college in Boston, and she developed a life-threatening illness.

HOPE: Nico called me from college and said, "My head feels like it's going to explode." I told her to go to an emergency room right away. When she went to the emergency room, they told her she had a sinus infection and sent her home with a decongestant. The symptoms kept getting worse, and she went back again. The doctor found a four-inch malignant tumor in her chest that was collapsing a vein in her neck. The cancer was a form of lymphoma that is very responsive to chemotherapy and radiation. I moved into the hospital with her in Boston until Laurence could get our house ready for a summer of chemotherapy and recovery.

LAURENCE: By Christmas her hair, which she had lost during chemotherapy, was coming back. She was able to return to college the next fall. It was an intense time for all of us. For Nico, it was daunting to face a life-threatening disease at only nineteen. That's the age when children are supposed to be moving toward independence from their parents. She was very sick and scared, and she needed to depend heavily on us.

HOPE: And in other ways, she matured beyond her years as a result of having to face death so early in life. She was told that she would need shots of blood thinner straight into her abdomen three times a day. They wanted to teach me how to administer them, but she wouldn't accept that. She insisted that she needed to know that, when I approached her, it was going to be for comfort, so she learned to do this for herself.

The stress of having an ill child did not create tension between Laurence and me. We were a comfort to each other throughout the ordeal. We remained purposeful, coordinating our team effort, taking one step at a time. I am grateful to have a solid connection that allows us to handle stress so gracefully.

LAURENCE: When I had to be in Germany for work during the time that Nico was recovering, I totally trusted Hope to handle things well without me. Nico is fine now, thank goodness, so we are no longer preoccupied with her health issues.

As artists, we find it hard to have genuine objectivity about our own work. We need to rely on each other's opinions. We're lucky to have just the right balance of safety and challenge. We have the idea of encouragement down, and playfully challenge each other constantly. If I'm writing a piece of music, Hope has a sense of where the magic is. When she's writing her scripts, I know what feels right and I tell her so. We're both clear that being an artist is not a job, it's a way of life.

A great relationship is an ongoing work of art

HOPE: I see our relationship as an art form. There's a lot of give and take and no absolutes. We know that conflict comes from rigidity and attachment. There is no good and bad, no right or wrong. There is just this interplay that has a lot of flux. I have the ability to open up my mind and let bright ideas fall in, which is a great gift, but it leaves me vulnerable too. I sometimes take in more than is good for me. I am naturally empathic, and my friends all call me when they're in trouble. I'm not thick skinned, and I've had to learn how to deal with criticism. That remains a continuing challenge for me.

LAURENCE: There is a popular notion that artists have to suffer to create their art. Neither of us subscribes to this belief. We believe that you can live in joy and happiness and be creative. This is truly our experience. For us, magic happens on a daily basis. Every day is rejuvenation. We are constantly looking for and finding the magic in the mundane, and we see it everywhere.

Surprise and unpredictability keep the sexual spark alive and well

LAURENCE: A lot of people think it's inevitable that, over time, you lose the sexual spark and romance leaves the marriage. That hasn't been the case for us. We're always surprising each other, and sometimes it feels that we're together for the first time, as though we've never seen each other before. It never feels old or stale between us, and I am no less turned on by Hope than I've ever been. I still appreciate attractive women, but I have no desire to have an affair. We're always having affairs with each other. It's a kind of paradox, to know someone so intimately and, at the same time, to constantly be surprised by how she shows up and what she brings. Living our life and our relationship as a creative project keeps everything fresh and alive and interesting almost all the time.

HOPE: We've just come out of our twenty years of hard-core parenting. Now that the children have left home, we're having a second honeymoon. We look for every opportunity to lift up the mundane parts of life to the level of magic. If I could clone Laurence, my friends would line up. They all want him, and I can see why. I still think he's the sexiest guy around. He's gorgeous; he's got those lovely green eyes and that melting English accent. And he's in love with me. It just doesn't get any better than this.

20.

LOVE GROWS EVERY TIME IT IS EXPRESSED

Pearl and Seymour Dychtwald

Many young people fear they will be trapped in a marriage that has become stale, predictable, and boring. The term *commitment-phobic* often refers to a terror of being stuck in a lifeless relationship that leaves both partners empty, resentful, or both. Pearl and Seymour Dychtwald are living proof that such a fate is not inevitable, and that love, passion, and vitality can continue to grow even when a couple has been together for nearly seven decades.

When we asked Ken and Maddy Dychtwald if they knew another couple who might be appropriate for our study, they both immediately suggested Seymour and Pearl. "My parents would be perfect for your book," Ken told us. "They have been married for sixty-five years and are still madly in love."

Unlike many retired couples whose lives and interests have narrowed down to a small number of friends and activities, the Dychtwalds continue to live on a broad playing field. For them, now well into their eighties, life is still very much about play. Not play in the literal sense of amusing activities, but play in the sense of approaching all of life's circumstances with an open mind and a desire to experience learning, fun, and engagement with others. Seymour and Pearl say they stay youthful and vital "by continuing to do the things we love to do." One of those things is to affirm their love for each other, which they do on a daily basis. They have been doing this for decades, and they never tire of it. An essential aspect of their play is to come up with new and creative ways to demonstrate their love.

The Dychtwalds were definitely not made with the same cookie cutter, and over the years they've become not more like each other but more themselves. They appreciate their differences and are thankful for them. According to Pearl, "It's not despite our differences that we have succeeded in creating such a rich life together, but because of them."

Our earliest experiences can shape our deepest commitments

PEARL: Although we have spent about 99 percent of the past sixty-two years together, the first three years of our marriage were quite different. Seymour was twenty-one when we got married in 1942, and I was eighteen and just out of high school. We were a couple of kids. Six months after our wedding, he joined the army, and three months after that he was sent to China, where he was stationed until 1946. Being separated for so long was difficult for me. I missed him terribly. I lived with my family while he was overseas, but the pain of our separation was great. When Seymour finally came home, I was overwhelmed with happiness. I didn't want to be separated ever again, and that's pretty much the way it's been ever since. That three-year separation was painful for us both, but the experience provided a powerful lesson about the preciousness of our connection and our desire to do whatever was necessary to sustain and deepen it.

SEYMOUR: We stayed in very close touch while I was away. We wrote to each other every single day, although sometimes, I admit, I would write two or three letters in a day and then mail them out one day at a time. Of course there were no emails in those days, and you couldn't make telephone calls, so those letters were our lifelines. Between the two of us, we wrote over two thousand.

Before I went overseas, I had worked with my brother running a gas station. He assured me that I would be a partner after I returned, but he reneged on his promise. I was really upset, but it forced me to start my own business, which turned out to be a very good thing. I opened up a dress shop, and it quickly became successful. I was determined to have the best dress shop in town, the best quality clothes, best prices, and best service. That was my goal, and I achieved it.

PEARL: Like most members of the Depression-era generation, we grew up with an acute sensitivity to money matters and were driven to earn enough money to provide for the family, which, by 1950, included our two sons, Ken and Alan. Seymour's immediate business success prompted him to open another shop, and then another. In less than ten years, he was operating six stores, all of them thriving. I was also involved in the business and was the manager of one of the stores.

SEYMOUR: I knew Pearl was very smart, and I wanted her to be involved with the business too, but I knew that if we worked together it could be a disaster. Pearl is very easygoing, but I like to be in control of things. The only way it would work for us was if she had her own store and I had nothing to do with it. I didn't trust myself not to meddle in things. She did a great job of running the business.

PEARL: I managed the store in Elizabeth, New Jersey. I hired personnel and supervised them. We paid our staff very well, much more than the going rate for sales help, so we were able to get the most knowledgeable and skilled people. The average pay at the time was around two dollars an hour, and we paid ten dollars. Some people thought we were crazy paying that much, but we knew what we were doing and it was definitely the right thing. Our staff loved working for us, and we had very little turnover. We're still friendly with many of those people who worked for us years ago.

SEYMOUR: My one regret is that I didn't spend more time with the boys. I was so determined to build a successful business that I left most of the child-rearing responsibilities to Pearl. She's always been a wonderful mother, the best, really. I couldn't ask for a better mother for my sons. She's steady, patient, and very loving. I didn't really think about spending more time at home then. It was a different world. Men didn't get so involved with the family back then. Seeing how involved with his family my son Ken is now, what a devoted father he is, has made me realize how important that is and what I missed and what the boys missed. Fortunately their mother made up for my absence, but still, if I had to do it over again, knowing what I know today, I'd have spent more time at home. In some ways, I think, I'm making up for it by my involvement with our grandchildren.

It's never too late to make up for what you missed

PEARL: Even though three thousand miles separate us from the grandchildren, we are very involved grandparents. Our granddaughter, Casey, and grandson, Zak, are now twenty-five and twenty-two. We love them so much, and they honored us by officiating on the occasion of our sixtieth-anniversary remarriage. We exchanged vows again and pledged and affirmed our love in front of friends and family. Lots of tears of joy and gratitude were flowing on that day.

SEYMOUR: Even though I retired from the family business in 1987, I maintain an extremely active life. Among other things, I have been coeditor of a local newspaper and director of a couples' golf tournament for fourteen years. I have lectured to senior citizen groups on finance, current events, and other subjects of interest. I had been an avid reader, subscribing to several daily newspapers and a number of weekly and monthly magazines. I wrote a lot of letters to the editor, many of which got published.

PEARL: In 2003, all of that changed. Seymour developed macular degeneration in his left eye, and his doctor suggested surgery to correct his vision. Rather than restoring vision to his bad eye, the surgery resulted in a loss of vision in the good eye as well. He has virtually no possibility of recovery of sight in either eye. He is legally and permanently blind.

SEYMOUR: I'm now unable to drive, read, watch movies, or do most of the things I used to love to do. Yet there's so much I can still do because of Pearl. She's become my eyes. She helps me find things, drives me places, and takes care of me in ways that make me feel that my life is still good, that I'm still a productive and worthwhile human being. The biggest problem that I have with Pearl these days is that she does too much for me. I wish she wouldn't spend so much time and energy fussing over me and would do more of the things she likes to do. She has a lot of interests and activities in her life. I keep telling her that she doesn't have to sacrifice herself for me.

PEARL: I am doing what I want to do. This is what I want to do. Caring for you is what brings me happiness and fulfillment. I'm not sacrificing my other interests. I'm still doing them. I'm just helping you too!

SEYMOUR: [After a long pause] Thank you. Pearl's the giver; I'm the taker. I'm the loudmouthed, opinionated one. She's the good listener.

PEARL: It's his personality. He's always been this way; I really don't mind. Oh, there have been times when I've been frustrated with Seymour because he wasn't listening to me or he was upsetting me for some other reason, but I'd usually come up with some way to get through to him.

SEYMOUR: Like when you dumped the bowl of water on my head?

PEARL: I don't even remember what I was upset about, but I was angry, and I just picked up a big bowl of water and poured it over his head.

SEYMOUR: That got my attention. Pearl's easygoing, but don't let that fool you. She's got plenty of spirit too.

PEARL: If something is very important to me, I always find a way to get my point across.

SEYMOUR: While Pearl was unmistakably the primary parent of the family, and I was the breadwinner, she was and has continued to be much more than a good mother and supportive wife. In addition to having been a key player in the family business and manager of one of our most successful stores, she has another talent that has served her, and through which she has served many others. She is a professional dancer.

PEARL: I was trained in ballet as a child. It soon became evident that I had some natural ability. I became proficient in tap dance and modern dance and, while still a teenager, was hired by the Roxie Theater in New York City to be a chorus line dancer. I absolutely loved it. We traveled all over the country and performed in dozens of cities. I've always loved to dance and still do. I've never stopped. One of the ways that I give back to my community is by teaching tap dance to the other senior ladies, some of whom are in their nineties.

It's not enough to say "I love you"

PEARL: We both agree that it's not enough to just say "I love you," which we do on a daily basis to each other and other family members. We also stress the importance of displaying love through acts of kindness, caring, and generosity.

SEYMOUR: Ken helped me to appreciate the need to include others in our giving, in addition to the immediate family. He helped me see how important it is to give back to our community in response to all we've received. We've been blessed in so many ways.

PEARL: In addition to the many blessings we've received, we've also had our share of difficulties and challenges. One of the things that drove Seymour to focus so intently on earning a good living for his family had to do with his growing up in a very poor family during the Depression.

SEYMOUR: My father left us when I was seven years old. He just up and left, and we never heard from him again. I didn't know if he'd ever come back home or not. I kept hoping, but he never did. It was hard. I was the youngest of four boys, the baby. My nickname was "Bop" because my brother used to bop me on the head all the time. I started working for pennies when I was just a kid. I was glad to get whatever I could. I guess I just decided that I would work hard enough that my sons wouldn't have to go through what I did. When I look at my boys, I'm so proud of them. I wish I could have been the kind of father that Ken is.

In 2001, I was diagnosed with bladder cancer. I was eighty years old and also had high blood pressure and diabetes. The treatment has been successful, and the cancer has been in remission ever since. The side effects from the treatment severely impaired my ability to perform sexually. Up until that time, Pearl and I always had a passionate and active sex life. Now all of a sudden that's history. Although I obviously feel the loss of my sexual potency, my overall response to this change in life is one of acceptance. The way I've come to see it is that I experienced more than six decades of healthy sexuality, and there are a lot of other ways of being intimate and close besides sex. Pearl and I kiss and hug and cuddle every day. We make love and share love every day. That's what's most important to me. And Pearl never made fun of me or made me feel bad when things changed. I never for an instant felt any less loved or appreciated by her, and it never seemed like it was ever a problem for her either.

PEARL: As far as I'm concerned, it didn't change the quality of our life together, and it helped us share our love in ways that enriched and deepened our connection. It was never a problem for me. One of the ways that Seymour has come up with is by leaving love notes on the windshield of my car.

SEYMOUR: I started doing it a few years ago when I spotted her car in the parking lot at the country club when Pearl was playing golf. I got a kick out of imagining her coming back to her car and finding that note on the windshield, seeing her smile as she read it.

Shortly after my health crisis, we were faced with a crisis of a different type when the stock market took a big hit in 2001. The stocks that we had been holding lost much of their value. For the first time in almost fifty years, I was worried about not having enough money to keep us for the rest of our lives. I was really worried that we might be in serious financial trouble. For a period of time I couldn't sleep at night — I was up worrying about what we were going to do.

PEARL: I was never that worried about the finances. I knew that if worse came to worse, we could make some adjustments in our lifestyle and cut back on some of the luxuries we had grown accustomed to, without making any extreme sacrifices. It was just a matter of scaling back. We both knew how to live on less. We'd done it before, and if we needed to, we'd do it again. I wasn't worried.

Love is a choice strengthened by goodwill and caring actions

SEYMOUR: We are still very much in love. The flame of romance has not only continued to burn brightly but is stronger than ever. We don't just say "I love you," we show it in every imaginable way at every opportunity. We are still enjoying our life together tremendously. We stay very busy. If I had advice to give young people today, it would be to love and respect each other always. And remember that love isn't just about the physical. It's my wife's kind personality that makes me love her.

PEARL: And don't forget to remind each other of what you admire about him or her. Marriage is something you have to work at. You can't take the other person for granted. You can't just expect that because you're married, you don't have to continue to be as loving and attentive as you were before the wedding. Expressing my love to Seymour makes me love him more. Don't hold back. It's important to show interest in what your spouse is interested in.

SEYMOUR: And praise your spouse's good points. Don't focus on any negative qualities. Emphasize the positive. Oh, and don't forget to have fun.

21.

GREAT MARRIAGES REQUIRE A COMMITMENT TO SOMETHING BEYOND THE RELATIONSHIP ITSELF

Shakti and Rick Butler

S hakti and Rick Butler describe their marriage as a structure to support their lives and work and as a means to a greater end. They explain that the support provided by their relationship enables them to contribute on a grand scale to the fulfillment of their shared purposes. Both are committed to using their energy to bring about a world of greater respect, understanding, and integrity. As people of color, they have experienced more than their share of prejudice, and both grew up determined to confront the shadow of American culture by illuminating and addressing racism in its many forms. Both are filmmakers, and they have directed and produced many films that deal with issues of racism and diversity, some of which have won national awards.

Their beautiful and simple home in the Oakland Hills, with its stunning views of the San Francisco Bay, serves as a haven for friends, particularly young people who don't have stable living situations. It's a vital place infused with energy and spirit. During our visit with them, it was difficult for us to distinguish their own children from the others who flowed through their home. "Yeah, this is pretty much how it is around here most of the time," Shakti said to us. "It can get pretty chaotic, but even though it may not be apparent, we do have conditions that we require our family to meet. Those limits are more tolerant and lenient than in most families. What's most important to us is that the kids who spend time here, whether it's a few hours, a few months, or a few years, feel accepted, respected, and loved, and that they treat others in our home with respect."

The sanctuary that Shakti and Rick have established is much more than the physical structure of their home. It includes their relationship, which is characterized by great mutual respect and a deep commitment to social justice. Their shared desire to make this world a better place is an orientation to all life, and it's evident in their actions as well as their words. This commitment doesn't protect them from life's difficulties and ordeals; in fact, it seems to draw challenging situations to them.

Shakti and Rick didn't simply commit to staying together: they committed to creating the best relationship they could possibly have. As Rick tells us, the strength that has grown out of their willingness to invite and confront life's ordeals allows them to meet their challenges with grace and effectiveness. As their story reveals, when you follow your heart, the path may not be easy, but you'll find the help you need along the way.

SHAKTI: For practically as far back as I can remember, I've always been a spiritual seeker. My father's grandmother was Arawak Indian and the eighth daughter of a shaman. Because there were no sons, she was initiated as a healer. She tried on different religions like someone trying on many different pairs of shoes. She was a Seventh-day Adventist, a Baptist, a Catholic, and several others. Her husband, my grandfather, had been a slave in Texas and, after emancipation, went to Barbados in the West Indies, where he met and married my grandmother. She taught him to read and write. My father was born in 1890 and had a tremendous influence upon me. As a young man, he moved to New York. He was a poet, a mathematical genius, and a salesperson for Madam C. J. Walker, the first black female millionaire. He was also a professional boxer for a while, and his professional name was "One Punch Leroy." He owned a speakeasy, played piano for Billie Holiday, and was the first black Teamster ever hired in New York City. He also corresponded with Eastern meditation masters. He taught me how to meditate and had a profound influence on the development of my spiritual life.

My mom and dad met in a camp for political progressives in the forties. My mother's parents were Russian Jews and my father was probably the first black man she'd ever talked to. My mother came from a very poor working-class family. When she married my dad, most of her family disowned her. And so I grew up in Harlem, very much a part of black culture and traditions.

RICK: My father made a lasting impression on me, but in a very different way. I grew up in Pittsburgh. Both of my parents were the first in their families to go to college. My mother got an MA; my father became an MD, the first African American dermatologist in Detroit. He was an incredibly successful doctor, but he and my mother didn't get along, and they divorced when I was ten months old. My father maintained only occasional contact with the family after the divorce, and I was never close to him, at least not until the end of his life, when I was finally ready to give up my anger toward him. I was hurt and livid that he'd left us, and I had refused to forgive him. Our home wasn't warm; it was cold and angry, and that's how I became. I was always angry as a kid; I used to throw temper tantrums. My mother used to take us to church on Sunday — we were Presbyterians, but it was more of a social thing than anything else. I never got into it, though I knew, even when I was little, that there was something beyond the material world. I've felt a spiritual connection my whole life, but the church didn't really meet my spiritual needs, and it wasn't until I met Shakti that I began to understand the difference between religion and spirituality.

Not until we forgive someone can we appreciate the gifts they've given us

RICK: As my spiritual connection deepened, I became a more open, compassionate person. When my father retired from his practice after fifty-two years, at the age of seventy-nine, I felt closer to him than I had during my whole life. Our reconciliation let me appreciate more fully some of the gifts my parents gave me, which I had taken for granted or never really acknowledged.

My mother was politically conscious, particularly in regard to racial issues. I remember that we all attended the march on Washington in 1963. I was just a kid, but that experience had a profound effect on me. My political consciousness has informed much of the work I've done as a filmmaker.

SHAKTI: After I finished school, I got a job teaching in a school for handicapped kids in the South Bronx. It was a tough neighborhood, and the work was hard, but I loved it. I'd work all day, and at night I'd go out and party. I knew spiritually that there was something wrong with this picture, but I kept it up, staying too busy to take the time to examine my life. Underneath it all, I knew things were unraveling. By the age of twenty-three, I had had three abortions and some really hard times behind me. I moved to California shortly after turning thirty, intending to break my destructive patterns and get a new start. And that's exactly what happened. By the time I met Rick, I had one failed marriage behind me, and two kids, and had been drug free for several years.

RICK: I'd been doing drugs and alcohol since I was in high school. I didn't actually consider myself an addict, but I had no desire to give it up. When Shakti and I met, I was more certain that I wanted this woman in my life than I had ever been about anything. I had just gotten divorced for the second time, after nearly ten years of marriage. It had taken me a long, agonizing year to conclude that that marriage was over. I had been depressed and in a funk. My daughter was thirteen at the time, and I realized I needed to pull myself out of this funk for her sake.

I called my friend Baron and told him I just had to get out and get reengaged with life. Baron and I went to a club that very night and, unbeknownst to me, he had also invited Shakti to come along. We hit it off the instant we met. It was grace working through Baron that brought us together. We talked and talked and talked because we had so many things to say to each other. My whole mood changed that night.

SHAKTI: The night we met, I told Rick I was taking my two kids to the zoo the next day. He said he had a teenage daughter who was looking for a babysitting job, so we decided we would all go to the zoo together. We laughed so much, and Rick felt like a comfortable old shoe. We really fit. I wasn't looking for a relationship, but Rick enchanted me.

On day three, he finally kissed me. It was delicious. On day five, he said, "We might as well get married." I was divorced with two young children when I met Rick. My life was very full with my kids, my work, and my spiritual practice, so at first I wasn't sure about marrying him. A new relationship at a time when my spiritual life was opening up seemed like it could be an obstacle to the process. I see now that meeting Rick was an essential aspect of my spiritual growth. I went into a state of deep meditation and asked my teacher, Gurumayi Chidvilasananda for a sign. In that meditative state, I received an unmistakable affirmation that it was right for me to go ahead with this relationship.

RICK: I had been a film major at Stanford, and began working as a cameraman shortly after college. I've been a director since 1999, and both Shakti and I are filmmakers. Our commitment to social justice drives our work — we are deeply sensitive to issues of race and how racism is a destructive force in our culture. And we are passionately interested in personal and cultural transformation. We want to know everything there is to know about how change happens, and to make sure we are doing our part to move that process along as quickly as possible. We make films that call people to action. Our work and our private lives are completely intertwined — most of our conversations that are not about the kids are about politics and race. We're constantly discussing and debating. We don't see everything eye to eye, though; there are places where we agree to disagree.

SHAKTI: Rick is really gifted at what he does. He also has a lot of humility. You could talk to him for days and never find out that he's won four Emmy awards. I do all the bragging for him. He's generous, thoughtful, politically aware, and is a man of high integrity. He's solid as a rock. He supported me for ten years while I got my PhD in transformative learning. He loves me unconditionally, and I revel in that.

RICK: We have a mutual admiration society going here, because I believe Shakti is a saint. She's intuitive and is the warmest and most giving person on the planet. She doesn't say no; she just keeps giving. And not only to me. If there is a kid in need or a friend who is in trouble, she's right there to help. In our first days together, we both realized we were a good fit; and I've been basking in that love ever since.

Since both of us had divorces in our history, we knew we had a few things to learn about marriage if this one was going to be different. We wanted to make it work, but we also knew that wanting this wouldn't necessarily be enough.

SHAKTI: Early on in our relationship, we got involved in personal growth work and human potential training to strengthen ourselves and our bond. We got into a couples' group with six other couples, and we met together for years on a regular basis. The work we've both done on ourselves is what's enabled us to maintain the high quality of our connection. It's not that we never get hurt, angry, or upset with each other, but we've learned to keep showing up when we feel these things. We keep telling the truth no matter what.

The more you open your heart, the bigger your family

SHAKTI: All my life, I've dreamed of having a big house full of kids. My dream has come true. Rick and I raised our own three children, and now we are raising our grandchild. Over the years, we've had seven other children living with us whom we've raised or helped raise. Some stayed with us for a few months, others for several years — our house has always been one of those houses that all the neighborhood kids come to. We never turn anyone away, and all seem to feel welcome here. They stay as long as they need to and then move on, and we always stay in touch with them after they leave.

RICK: We have a boy living with us now who's a gifted dancer. This kid lives to dance. He's in his last year of high school and is planning to enter college next fall. We're like foster parents to the children who come to us, but we don't get any money from the state. We do make a financial contribution in the form of food and shelter, along with a lot of good advice, but we don't try to be their parents. We feel it's our responsibility to share what we have, because we've been gifted with so many resources. We have pretty lax house rules and only one requirement: they each have to pay it forward. Someday, others will come into their lives who will be in need, so we ask that they keep alive the tradition of supporting those in need.

SHAKTI: But our life hasn't always felt this abundant. There was a time when we lost everything financially and were actually homeless for six months. We had to give up our lovely home because it was too expensive, and we didn't have any money to pay rent. We moved into the home of one of our friends, along with our three kids.

RICK: We got into this situation because we had both become tired of the work we were doing professionally, and a marketing opportunity had come along. I didn't have sales experience, but Shakti did, and we decided to go for it. We both worked very hard for two years, and for several months we made some good money. But by that time, we began to see some flaws in the product we were selling, and flaws in the system we were part of. Shakti actually saw the lack of integrity in this organization before I did, and she withdrew. Because of my tendency toward blind tenacity, I wanted to continue with the business, but one day I just couldn't do it anymore.

SHAKTI: We went into a business we saw as an opportunity, but things went sour despite how hard we worked. We couldn't cover our expenses, and things quickly fell apart. At this time, our eighteen-year-old unmarried daughter found out she was pregnant. My mother had been living with us, and I had to let her go live with a friend of hers. I called my friend Karen, who had lived with us, along with her kids, when she got divorced, and told her that I was moving my family into her house. She didn't hesitate, and she took Rick and me and our three children, and even our dog, into her home. It was not a big house. The three children slept in sleeping bags on the floor, and I cried every single day for four months. It was really hard. I felt so guilty, like it was entirely my fault. I felt that I had coerced Rick into joining me in the financial world, when he's a gifted artist, not a businessman. I felt I had been carried away by greed.

RICK: I never blamed Shakti. I freely chose to try the business venture — it was a joint decision. We have had a policy of no blame since the beginning; we were being tested. We were both so grateful for the spiritual practice we had undertaken over the years. It taught us a lot about equanimity. When you have the right understanding, you have the same response to both pleasure and adversity.

SHAKTI: We passed the test. Our bond was strong, and it got even stronger. I eventually got my strength back, we found other work, and we got some cash flow going. During the months that we lived with Karen and her children, we all got so close that Karen became an aunt to our kids, and Rick and I became honorary aunt and uncle to hers. It's actually more like Karen's kids are our kids. My response to adversity is always to immediately ask "What is the lesson here? What is the universe trying to teach me? How can I grow from this?"

RICK: I've always known that give-and-take is required for a good relationship. I tend to be headstrong, but I've learned that it can be disastrous in a close relationship. I've learned to relinquish something for the sake of depth. There is a time and place to be strong-willed and independent, and a time to be soft and dependent. I know that as I develop a stronger sense of myself I can merge more closely with Shakti in a healthy way. I no longer have to keep myself so separate, because I've come to understand that I can merge with her without losing myself.

SHAKTI: It's like a dance where the music changes. It's subtle. For me, it's the capacity to keep showing up even when I'm afraid. There are times when I'm in uncharted territory where I lose my voice. My first reaction when I'm afraid is to blame someone, but I don't stay there long. I have trained myself to become responsible fast. I never stay angry for long anymore. It was that commitment we made early in our relationship — to keep learning and growing — that has worked for us. The many classes, workshops, and couples groups we've taken part in have helped us become more responsible.

RICK: I feel closer to Shakti now, after nineteen years together, than I ever have. I know I'm a survivor, and that I wouldn't make it without her in my life. We rely deeply on each other, and we are each self-reliant. We're very much our own selves, and at the same time we're deeply connected and interdependent. That connection has made all that we've created possible. Getting here hasn't always been easy, but it's been worth every bit of the effort. Well worth it.

22.

CHANGE YOUR LIFE, CHANGE YOUR MARRIAGE, CHANGE THE WORLD BY LISTENING, REALLY LISTENING

Michael and Justine Toms

Michael and Justine birthed the *New Dimensions* radio program and began broadcasting locally from a small studio at KQED-FM in San Francisco in 1973. The very small listenership they attracted with a single station thirty-six years ago has grown to a worldwide audience that now numbers in the millions. Syndicated to more than six hundred stations worldwide, *New Dimensions* airs weekly and features cutting-edge teachers, social architects, scientists, creative artists, and other visionaries of our time.

After beginning with a concept that Michael and Justine jointly created, the current reality they share is far greater than anything either of them imagined three and a half decades ago. Having created thousands of hours of recorded dialogues with such luminaries as Krishnamurti, Buckminster Fuller, Joseph Campbell, Maya Angelou, and His Holiness the Dalai Lama, these two continually fulfill the *New Dimensions* mission: to explore the furthest reaches of our personal and collective human possibilities as a means of promoting global transformation.

Much of Justine and Michael's collected wisdom has come from their own life challenges. Perhaps one of the most powerful lessons they have absorbed has been to learn from their own experiences and always honor the truth of their hearts. They stand as a strong example of the creative and healing power of a committed partnership. We felt their warmth, humor, and insight into themselves and their relationship during the entire time we spent with these two world-class interviewers. We left the interview more certain than ever that the support of a loving partner can get you through times of unspeakable pain and difficulty, and that it can also make miracles happen.

A real man is strong *and* tender, and so is a real woman

JUSTINE: Michael was thirty-three when we met, and I had just turned thirty. It was at a big dinner party hosted by some mutual friends. I was struck by the gentle man who hadn't wanted to leave his new kitten at home and so brought this furry ball with him. "Donald" was sitting on Michael's shoulder when we were first introduced. I was so touched by the tenderness of this big guy caring for a tiny kitten.

MICHAEL: Justine was beautiful, and I immediately found myself drawn to her. I remember thinking, "Why can't I find a woman like this?"

JUSTINE: At the beginning of our relationship, I told Michael I wanted to get to know him better, but first of all we had to talk about spiritual things. I thought I'd show him the light and win him over to my religion, so I came over to his house armed with all my Jehovah's Witnesses books, including their translation of the Bible. I told him I wanted to talk about the Bible and I wanted to use my translation. Michael reached back to one of his shelves of books and pulled out the New World translation of the Bible, the very one I had been using. What I didn't realize was that he had an entire shelf of translations of the Bible.

I remember thinking to myself, "Maybe he's more inclusive than I am," but I quickly dismissed that thought and plunged in, relating to him my different interpretations of some verses in the New Testament. Michael said, "I hear what you are saying, but you might want to look at it like this." He never said, "You are wrong; this is the right way to interpret that text." Every time he spoke, rather than negating my view he seemed to include my view in a landscape bigger than the one I was looking at. I came to understand that what I was actually going for was not the dogma of religion but larger spiritual truths. I was looking for the biggest truth I could find. That night we fell in love. It was the start of my stretching to include other points of view, and it was really the beginning of our work together as well.

MICHAEL: Nine months later we started *New Dimensions*. We continue to have the same kind of conversation, only now we have microphones and everyone can be part of the dialogue. It was our own personal quest for truth that sparked our work together. We knew right from the beginning that this work was bigger than the two of us.

JUSTINE: When we first started working together, I was very shy. When it came to meeting famous people, I had trouble getting out of the house to go to the studio.

MICHAEL: I could see how reluctant Justine was, but I also saw who she was. She couldn't see it in herself. I would say, "Come on, Justine, you don't have to do very much. Would you be willing to just greet the guests? You don't have to do the interview; I'll handle that."

JUSTINE: So I would meet the guests at the door and invite them in. I could simply be a hostess making conversation. I felt I could at least do that much. Gradually, by degrees, I began to see who Michael had fallen in love with. He's always had a lot of confidence in me. He's always been a risk taker, and he has taught me a lot about stretching myself and taking risks.

MICHAEL: I felt it was of utmost importance for Justine to be in the studio, to make eye contact with me, and to keep the energetic connection between us strong. Justine has always been my muse. I almost never put anything out to the public before letting her see it first. I may have taught her about boldly stepping into the big outer world, but she has been a wonderful teacher who taught me about going into my inner world.

JUSTINE: Some years later, when Michael took a job with a national radio network, I agreed to take over as director of *New Dimensions*. I stipulated that I was willing to do everything but the finances.

Ironically, for most of the next three years, the finances turned out to be the major part of the business that I handled. I also did the marketing and found that I was good at it. Handling all these responsibilities so well gave me a huge boost in confidence. Once I had a stronger sense of myself, I was able to push Michael on to his own greatness. I could see his vast capacity for excellence, and I asked him to reach down deeper and to rev up the whole engine. That's when he comes up with his best work.

MICHAEL: When I returned to *New Dimensions*, I came back not only to a changed organization but also to a changed partner. Justine was so much more fully developed. I hadn't taken a salary out of the business for the first twenty years; I had other sources of income. We made sacrifices, but we were doing what we loved. Then *New Dimensions* began to thrive. I'm certain I have developed myself because Justine holds the bar of excellence high.

JUSTINE: Michael is never competitive with me. He is sufficiently secure to celebrate my empowerment, which is a great gift to our relationship. Our commitment to our relationship is strong, but our greatest commitment is to reach higher consciousness. When people look at us, they think it's wonderful and easy. But it's not so easy when there are health issues, losses, and decisions that have to be made, when he wants to zig left and I want to zag to the right. But it's our life path. Sometimes it's a grind, and sometimes it's pure joy.

There is such stress in keeping up in modern life. Just about everyone we know is rushing to keep up. In our relationship, we started at the top of the mountain and fell off. The stress of not having enough money was a serious problem for years that kept us from being our best. We continue to deal with this issue as the tides of change keep tossing us about, requiring us to re-create our business model.

MICHAEL: There were many times in the early days when we were so short of money that it was questionable whether there was even enough to buy groceries.

JUSTINE: On my birthday during one of our lean years, there wasn't enough money for Michael to buy me a gift. I was really hurt that he didn't get me a birthday present. And on top of feeling hurt, I felt ashamed that I was so disappointed. I considered keeping all this to myself — I was reluctant to be vulnerable. But I felt I was about to pop from carrying so much feeling. I opened up to Michael with "I have to tell you something, and I'm afraid that when you hear it you won't love me." And then I told him about my sorrow that he didn't buy me a gift.

MICHAEL: Knowing something about Justine's childhood, I said, "Of course you feel like that. You've had similar moments in your child-hood — your father traveled a lot, and when he was gone the house-hold would often fall apart. No groceries in the house, your mother absent in alcohol. Then your father would come back from his trips bringing presents. He would fill the whole car with groceries. These material things made you feel secure and loved."

JUSTINE: Telling Michael about my emotional reaction to financial stress combined with birthdays, both his and mine, was scary. But I felt compelled to reveal rather than conceal. Michael's insight into my process greatly encouraged me to continue being honest and to bring up anything, no matter how dark. This moment of truth-telling led to hundreds of others like it. When I was twelve, my father and little brother were killed in a plane crash. It was months before the crash site and their bodies were discovered. My family completely fell apart; it was just too much for my mother to handle. I was supposed to go on that plane trip with my dad. At the last minute, I didn't get to go, and my little brother went instead of me. A lot of grief and feelings had been put in the deep freeze, which I had to take out to thaw and warm by the fire of Michael's caring. It was in facing my demons and speak-ing them out loud to a caring, loving person that I let my demons dis-solve. I've done this over and over again, and each time I come out with my deep, dark, shadowy secrets, I feel lighter and more at peace.

MICHAEL: For Justine to simply tell me what she felt and needed, and to be met with understanding and care, was revolutionary. It created a new level of healing, not just in her family, but in mine as well. Over the years, we have become so very close, and our trust has deepened.

There is, however, a shadow side to such closeness and caring. It showed up one time when I wasn't feeling well. I was falling asleep in the middle of the day, gaining weight, and feeling terribly weak and tired. Every morning, Justine lovingly reported to me what she thought the problem was, and because my trust in her was so strong, I believed her.

JUSTINE: This was just before we were due to fly to Costa Rica on business. I could tell that Michael didn't really want to go, and I offered to go by myself so he could stay home to rest. As it turned out, my going without him was a lifesaver. When Michael found himself alone, without me reporting on how he was feeling, he started to do his own inner checking. In doing so, he realized he was in much worse shape than either of us had suspected. Only when I was away from him could he start to see clearly what he needed to do.

It's possible to trust someone too much

MICHAEL: During my morning meditation, I became aware that I had to decide whether to live or die. I chose life and drove myself to the emergency room. It turned out that I had pneumonia. They immediately put me on oxygen, even before they took any blood samples for lab work. I started recovering right away.

JUSTINE: It was a big wake-up call for me. Michael and I had become so close, and because of that closeness I thought I knew what was going on in his body. This is the shadow side of being so connected. We may believe we know certain things about the other person, but sometimes it's just arrogance on our part. I had assumed a responsibility that wasn't necessarily in Michael's best interest. Ever since this happened, I have encouraged Michael to better monitor his own health and not depend on me. He is the one who lives in his skin, not me.

MICHAEL: I learned a great deal from this incident too. I trusted Justine's intuition to the point where it almost killed me. I realized I was not taking responsibility for my own truth. I was overriding it and deferring to her. We both came through this wiser than before.

JUSTINE: When my mother was sick with cancer, we brought her to live in our home for six months, until she died. As you can imagine, it was an emotional time. Michael had the good sense to back off, because I had a whole process to go through. For a while, my libido vanished and I didn't have much energy to give him. I had to draw on my spiritual practice just to stay centered enough to get through this demanding period. I'm sure Michael could feel me distancing myself from him and everyone else, and I appreciated all the room he gave me. During that time, he demanded nothing of me.

MICHAEL: I backed way off because I saw this was needed. I put my energy into my work instead. The whole extended family was converging on our home.

JUSTINE: Michael and I have a great capacity to be separate as well as close. When we first got together, he told me right away that he would love me as much as he could love any woman, but that he had other things in his life that were important to him as well. I was so young and romantic back then that I was greatly disappointed. Before meeting Michael I was used to being the sun and the moon to my romantic partner. I was hurt, but at the same time I intuited that his additional commitments were of the deepest spiritual nature. It was the spiritual path that we were both committed to. During our years together, I've learned that the best relationships are not the ones where two people fall into one another. We develop stronger relationships when both partners stand straight and tall and love themselves, rather than ask the other to fill the bottomless well of longing to be loved.

MICHAEL: I sustained a great loss when my thirty-three-year-old son, Mike, took his own life. It was the only way out of his pain that my son could see. In his thirty-three years, he lived a very full life, because he went double time.

JUSTINE: When Mike's wife, Deanna, came over to tell Michael that his son had died by committing suicide, I was on the phone in the next room laughing with a friend. When I came into the room, I thought it was strange that she was here on a Sunday morning. Michael then seemed to just blurt out the words that Mike was dead. My immediate reaction was to want him to take the words back — as if he could undo it all by not saying these terrible words. It seemed so incongruous that I had been laughing with a friend only moments earlier, and now our entire lives were changed. I started saying over and over, "No, no, don't say it." Once I could pull myself together and be there for Michael, I realized there was no way anyone could prepare for such a thing. And I also realized that in one moment you could be blissfully happy and all is right with the world, and in the next instant, you could be caught in the worst grief and pain you've ever known. We never know what life has in store for us.

MICHAEL: Although the pain of losing a child is terrible, and suicide adds a layer of suffering, some gifts came from the tragedy. My son, Mike, had two children, Jeremy and Megan. My son went out of his way to see that I was at the birth of my grandson. I was the first person Jeremy saw when he opened his eyes. I have become so much closer to my grandchildren since Mike's death. It has been enormously healing for me; it has soothed the raw place left by my son's death, which tore him away from me. It's uncanny that I find myself in the exact same physical location, saying the same messages to Jeremy that I had said to Mike. I watch myself walk the razor's edge of sadness and joy. I have lost my fear of death. Justine and I have become closer; she was such a sustaining influence during my time of heavy grief.

I was so blasted open that I had to beg for help. It came in the form of the spirit of Our Lady of Guadalupe. I kept saying her prayer over and over: "I hold you in my arms. Give me your pain." I knew that I had to seek a deep spiritual presence. What I was experiencing was too big to put on Justine. I knew instinctively that I couldn't place something this huge at her feet, that she couldn't hold the pain for me. I had to go to the Great Mother, Mother Earth. It was a major turn in the road of life for me.

JUSTINE: For some couples, death can tax the relationship so heavily that they break up. This is often the case when a child dies. But for us, these things brought us closer together. When my mother died, Michael, in his quiet way, stood by me witnessing my process, and when it was my turn to stand by him, I did the same.

MICHAEL: We know that marriage is not the only way to enjoy a deeply fulfilling life, but for us it has brought riches unimaginable. Even though we laughingly call our committed relationship a "conscious crucible," we know that each of us has grown, and hopefully will continue to grow, in an ongoing practice of ever-deepening love.

23.

WHEN OUR UNDERLYING
INTENTIONS ARE ALIGNED, ALL
DIFFERENCES BECOME WORKABLE

Gay and Kathlyn Hendricks

Gay and Kathlyn Hendricks have long been considered experts in the field of relationships and body-mind integration. Between the two of them, they have authored or coauthored more than thirty-five books, several of them bestsellers. Married for more than twenty-five years, this couple began their relationship after each had learned some difficult but powerful lessons in previous marriages. They found in each other not only a spouse but also a life partner who could share their passion for learning, service, teaching, and spiritual growth, to a degree they had never previously experienced.

When we asked Gay and Kathlyn if there had been any challenging issues in their marriage, and if they'd be willing to share them, they were happy to talk about the one issue that, for years, had been the fly in the ointment that kept surfacing over and over again. Their story reveals that seemingly entrenched struggles need not be permanent despite a long and frustrating series of efforts to resolve them. The two of them remind us that a receptive mind is often more likely to resolve problems than long periods of intensive analytical thinking, and that a loving partnership can heal painful, long-standing emotional wounds. These two are the real deal.

Wealth is in the mind, not the bank account

GAY: In practically every aspect of our marriage, we've enjoyed a high degree of harmony and alignment, with one exception. For several years, despite our best efforts, it seemed impossible for us to get a grip on "the money thing." Everything else in our lives was great. We were teaching relationship courses, writing relationship books, and developing an international reputation as relationship experts, but this one piece of our lives was a persistent source of struggle and distress.

KATHLYN: It wasn't that we weren't earning much money. Plenty of it was coming in, but it just never seemed sufficient to cover all the bills. No matter how much we made, it never seemed to be enough. Aggravating the situation was the fact that we each had very different attitudes about money, and these were often incompatible. Any discussion about finance could easily become an intractable argument. Not surprisingly, we were both reluctant to even bring the subject up. Whenever one of us did, things would inevitably deteriorate into an argument or a shouting match, in which we would take turns criticizing the other for his or her "irresponsible" spending practices.

Don't recycle; break the cycle

GAY: Then one day, we experienced a real breakthrough. I was sitting on my exercise bike pedaling away and thinking about our finances, feeling the usual tension, when it occurred to me that the conversation playing over and over in my mind sounded familiar. I was cycling through my mind the very same fear — that our money wouldn't last until the end of the month — that had been playing in my mind for years.

Suddenly I realized that, before my adult mind had picked it up, this same conversation used to go on in my home as I was growing up. As I continued to pedal, I moved into a higher, expanded state, and it dawned on me that I could program my mind in a different way, that the conditioned pattern I had picked up in my family didn't work for me. I realized I could decide to think a new pattern into being, one in which we had enough money to do whatever we wanted. I'm not exactly sure what caused it, but suddenly I understood there was a more creative way to address this issue. We didn't have to remain in this state of stress anymore.

KATHLYN: At the time, we were both in our forties. For us, as it is for many people, money was such an important symbol of security, trust, and caring that it also became a source of fear and conflict for us. We would take turns criticizing each other for spending too much and putting our budget in a precarious position. At the time of Gay's realization, it was early spring, nearly tax season. In another room of the house, as if telepathically connected, I was bent over the checkbook, unable to breathe freely because of the tension in my body, attempting to pay the bills. Gay came bursting into the room and told me about his creative idea. He was completely convincing, and so enthusiastic about no longer having to waste energy worrying about money that he enrolled me in the idea. We made an agreement on the spot to let go of our scarcity orientation and consciously think in terms of abundance. We shook hands, pledging to be allies, rather than enemies.

GAY: It was a big turning point in our lives. We agreed to stop arguing about money, and we did. It was incredibly liberating. Our inner wisdom had been yelling at us to pay attention, and we finally began to notice how we spoke about money. We changed the language and began using more positive words. For instance, instead of saying, "We have some money," we began to say "We are enjoying plenty of money." We had been so uncomfortable with this issue that we were ready to come together as partners and make our alliance work in this domain as we had in other areas of our lives.

You can make your marriage a blame-free zone

KATHLYN: We had been stuck being enemies and were unable to express our creativity. Blaming Gay for mismanaging our money and expecting him to make me feel better was siphoning off valuable energy that we needed in order to create some cash and use it well. I could see so vividly in this instance how blame was a symptom of not using my creativity. We committed to creating a no-blame marriage. Whenever I noticed the grumbling, blaming voice in my mind, I immediately replaced it with the thought "How am I not using my creativity?"

GAY: As a result of the pact we made that day, money has become a nonissue in our lives. We have plenty of money, and we enjoy it! We don't worry about it anymore. We've found that things work the same way in any area of a relationship. The combination of two people using their energy together and lining up their commitments is powerful. It takes only ten minutes a day to focus on creativity and move out of scarcity. If people would do that for a week, and take a baseline reading of their vitality at the beginning of the week and then again at the end, they would see from their own experience how powerful such a focus can be.

KATHLYN: Responsibility and creativity are absolutely related. Whenever we give our power away to others, we abdicate our own creativity. When we take responsibility, we own our creativity. Resistance to claiming responsibility keeps us from moving forward. As I see it, I am the source of what happens. For me, it is moving out of the victim role and into the realm of creativity. This has been a big shift for me, because I came from an extremely critical family.

GAY: In the past, Kathlyn might hear a simple comment from me as criticism and would automatically become defensive. When she began to question her knee-jerk reactions and became curious, she released herself from her old, habituated patterns and could receive my loving attention. This didn't happen overnight. The process unfolded over a period of years. I would have to begin my remarks by saying, "This isn't criticism." Kathlyn would then stop to reassess her initial reaction and notice that my intention was not to be critical. In time, these interchanges helped her to heal. She began to hear my belief in her. I could see the beauty in her that she couldn't see, and reflect it back to her.

KATHLYN: One place this phenomenon showed up was when we started to teach classes together. It was a challenge for me because Gay seemed so experienced and at ease in his teaching, and I was convinced that he was taking up all the space. I would tell him I had to duck because he was so flamboyant and huge that there wasn't a place for me. I wanted him to move over so I could have some room to speak.

GAY: When Kathlyn complained to me about it, I told her, "There's plenty of space. I'm not going to slow down. If you want to step in, go ahead and step in."

KATHLYN: For me, it was like standing in a Zen monastery and being presented with a koan. I felt he'd told me something important and true, but I didn't know what he was talking about. Then I began to get curious about how I perceived Gay. The act of taking responsibility started with wondering, "How am I creating this? What is there for me to learn from this?" The only move I could make that had any power was to wonder.

I began to connect the dots and saw that I had projected my older brother onto Gay. My brother was called "Number One." Energetically, Gay was a lot like him, and our scenes reminded me of times in the past when I felt there wasn't room for me, that my big brother was taking up all the space. I was playing it out again, as if Gay were holding me back. This was an important turning point for me. I began asking, "What do I want? What can I contribute that is uniquely my own?" This led me to show up in a whole different way in the classes we taught together. I came to realize that Gay was inviting me to fully be myself. It is so much more fun to have a dance of two equals.

Too much analysis can lead to paralysis

KATHLYN: When I take ten minutes to access myself and then connect to Gay, problems disappear. When we're stuck, it's not important how we got to that place. We could talk about that forever, but it doesn't make any difference. What really matters in that small segment of time is to stay focused on what we're going to do about it right now. We often deliberately remember what we felt toward each other when we first met. The energy was so pure, so strong, so compelling, that just taking a moment to remember it can put things in perspective.

The negative energy starts to shrink, and the creative energy starts to expand.

GAY: We're much more interested in "what" and "how" questions, because they have so much more power than the "why" questions. "What" and "how" questions reflect our overriding commitment to taking total personal responsibility for creating what we want.

KATHLYN: I made a basic shift in my life when I became better able to love myself as I am. I used to be a super perfectionist. I was constantly comparing myself to an idealized version of the person I thought I was supposed to be, and driving myself to live up to that unrealistic ideal. I was unhappy because I continually fell short of my standard. My relationship with Gay has allowed me to unhook from perfectionism and focus instead on play and creativity.

GAY: And I have learned a great deal from Kathlyn about organization. In the past, I never gave much thought to many parts of life that need ongoing attention — from washing dishes to having a desk orderly enough that I didn't have to waste time searching for things. I could eat a sandwich in the middle of World War III, but I've learned the value of having an orderly environment. One of Kathlyn's many gifts is her ability to create beauty wherever she is. She finds ways to make wherever we live incredibly attractive. When we first met, I was oblivious to the idea of bringing beauty into a living situation, and my home at the time had nothing on the walls. Now that I am attuned to beauty, I get so much enjoyment from the flower arrangements she makes every day; they are good enough to win prizes. For Kathlyn, creating beauty is an everyday occurrence. It comes easily to her. I realize that I called Kathlyn into my life to help me to develop that part of myself.

Our commitment to spirituality and meditation for the last twenty-five years has been absolutely central to developing our bond. As a result of our practice, we both find that we have much more energy and more to give to the people and communities around us. Learning to be present in our meditation has allowed us to be more present with other people.

KATHLYN: When we meditate and practice being with what is, it spills over into the rest of our life, and we can use the same practice of making space for what is occurring.

GAY: So much of our work has to do with helping people uncover and express their hidden genius, the special qualities we all have that make us unique in the world. Because Kathlyn and I have experienced so much support from each other in this process, we're able to teach others. We know that when people express their genius, whatever that might be, life takes on a completely different quality. Things become efficient; there's no wasted energy, and there's a remarkable sense of ease and effortlessness.

24.

ABOVE ALL ELSE, LOVE
IS THE MOST IMPORTANT THING

Joyce and Barry Vissell

The story of lovers who come from different clans is as old as time. In the case of Barry and Joyce, having to choose between following their hearts and bending to conform to their families' values proved to be the first of many challenges that would strengthen their commitment to each other and to a life of spiritual service. Raised in different faiths, Barry and Joyce were certain that the strength of their love would be sufficient to overcome any complications that might arise from their different religious backgrounds. Both sets of parents, however, saw things differently.

Sometimes a couple must drop into the pits of hell to find the motivation and develop the strength to meet their challenges. At these times, nothing less than a fierce commitment will open the door to greater possibilities. The problem, of course, is that the door swings both ways, and what can inspire and intensify one person's commitment can break another's. Barry and Joyce not only survived this and other crises, but they also grew in their capacity to love and to open their hearts far beyond what either of them as twenty-five-year-olds could have imagined. Coauthors of seven books and workshop leaders for more than thirty years, Joyce and Barry have dedicated their lives to service, contribution, and spiritual growth. Their greatest lessons have come not from books or seminars but from the experiences that challenged them personally on the playing field of their own marriage.

JOYCE: Barry and I met when we were both eighteen and freshmen in college. We fell deeply in love immediately — neither of us had experienced anything like it before. But both sets of parents had a problem with our relationship. I come from a Protestant family, and Barry is Jewish, and this proved to be a major source of stress for our families. As much as we loved each other, it felt scary and disloyal to go against our parents' wishes. We were young, and we succumbed to the pressure, deciding it would be best for all if we broke off our relationship. We tore ourselves apart and said good-bye. It was one of the most painful experiences of my life. We were both overwhelmed with sadness and couldn't stop crying. It was awful.

BARRY: We were in different colleges. I was at Boston University; Joyce was at Columbia University in New York. We agreed to make a clean break of it and cut our tie completely, because otherwise the pain would have been unbearable. We stopped speaking to each other altogether. But despite our best efforts, neither of us could let go. Our love was too strong to let each other go. It felt like an impossible situation.

JOYCE: After weeks of being separated and missing each other, I went up to the roof of my dorm and prayed all night for spiritual guidance. I prayed for a sign that would show me what to do. The next day, a friend's mother visited from central Pennsylvania. She gave me a bookmark that had fallen out of her Bible. She told me, "The feeling that I should give this to you was so strong that I took the four-hour bus ride just to bring it to you today." The words on the bookmark were "Above all else, love is the most important thing." When I saw that, I knew I had received the answer to my prayers. I knew what I had to do. I called Barry and told him I knew we were meant to be together. He told me he felt the same way, and we both knew that our days of separation were over for good.

BARRY: Both families were disappointed when we got engaged. We married when we were twenty-two and I was in my first year of medical school. Although we were so happy to be together, this was not a particularly easy time. I was clear that I wanted to be a physician, but I was filled with worry about being in a white and Jewish minority in an African American medical school in the south in 1968.

I remember one day when I was at a low point, and I revealed my fear and vulnerability to Joyce. Up until that point in our marriage, I had not revealed much vulnerability and need for her love. This touched Joyce so deeply that she looked straight into my eyes with a penetrating gaze and said, "You are so beautiful. I am awed by your beauty." I was so utterly moved by her acknowledgment that I was no longer able to hold on to the limited view of myself that I had been carrying around for most of my life. I really experienced the truth of Joyce's belief in me. It was real. I knew I now needed to see the beauty within me, the beauty Joyce saw in that pivotal moment.

The path of devotion isn't for sissies

JOYCE: Then when we were both twenty-five, something happened that I was completely unprepared for. Barry had an affair with my best friend. Neither of us could conceal the truth in our relationship; I found out about the affair because Barry told me immediately after it happened. But what was worse than hearing about the affair was hearing Barry say he wanted to continue having sex with other women. I was so hurt and enraged that I felt like killing him. When Barry told me that he wanted an open marriage, a very large "No!" rose from deep within me. My instincts rose to the surface and very clearly let me know that this would never work for me. I had never felt so angry about anything before, and it terrified me. I felt as if I could physically harm him. I locked myself in our bathroom and stayed there all night. Early the next morning, I took our dog and left our home. I didn't think the situation was resolvable.

BARRY: I had never thought Joyce would leave me, and it put me in a state of shock. When the full impact of the situation hit me, I began to think of what life would be without her. The pain overwhelmed me. I saw more clearly how my actions had affected her. I also felt the depth of my love for her, and more important, saw how much I needed her. Prior to this episode, I had not been in touch with the little boy inside me who needed love, and having the affair was a feeble attempt to prove to myself that I didn't need her. I was grateful that the experience revealed this part of myself that had been hidden. I was grief-stricken at losing Joyce, and at the same time I felt admiration and respect for her integrity and strength.

JOYCE: As much as I loved Barry and was committed to him, I knew I had to honor myself too, and that I couldn't live in a sexually open marriage. I had to draw a clear boundary and stick with it, even if it meant losing Barry. In drawing that line I discovered strength I didn't know I had. A week after the affair with my friend, Barry asked to meet with me one more time. I reluctantly came to see him. He looked and acted differently, and it was clear he had experienced a great deal of pain and suffering.

BARRY: I told Joyce that I recognized and accepted my need for her. It had never been all right for me to need anyone, and allowing myself to feel my need for her healed something deep within me. I no longer had to act out with other women, and I wanted us to come back together in a new and different way.

JOYCE: I left that day in silence. My resolve to end the marriage was shaken, and I spent the next several days reflecting on what I was feeling. One week later we again came together and committed ourselves to rebuilding our marriage. It was clear to both of us that we needed a monogamous relationship. We also saw that we needed to stop all drug and alcohol use to be as clear as we possibly could be.

You can't hurry trust

BARRY: It took two years to rebuild trust after the affair. Although I wished Joyce could get over her mistrust more quickly, I knew I couldn't rush the process, that it would take time for her to heal. I learned to develop patience and compassion. It was a difficult but valuable time for me. There were many moments when Joyce's mistrust resurfaced. At those times, when she spoke of her pain and doubt, I would meet her with the strength of my conviction by saying, "I trust that I have changed, and I hope that some day you will trust that too." I held Joyce in my arms without trying to change her or take away her fears.

JOYCE: Barry's allowing me to have my feelings, and his steadfast reassurance, helped me regain trust, and it came back stronger than ever. I saw that he now held me in higher regard than he ever had. His respect helped me feel deeper respect for myself. Barry's affair forced us to create a new relationship within the existing one.

The most important lesson from that experience was that we needed a common spirituality. It wasn't going to work for me to attend the temple or for Barry to attend church with me; we needed to find a spirituality that would bless both of us. We started on a long journey of spiritual exploration and discovered the common thread in all religions and spiritual paths, the presence of love. Striving to live with the awareness of this great presence has been the foundation of our relationship. Drawing on this presence has brought us to thirty-nine years of marriage, three children, and our work in healing relationships, which we absolutely love. Our relationship now rests firmly on a spiritual foundation that blesses our lives. We both agree that the regular practice of prayer is the most important part of each day for us.

BARRY: Joyce's statement that prayer is an important part of our day is an understatement. Our commitment to embody our spiritual principles is the centerpiece of our lives, our work, and our relationship. Like many of the other challenges we faced over the years, the crisis that nearly ended our relationship before it began strengthened our relationship and our spiritual connection. The religious differences that initially caused us and our families great anguish ultimately proved to be the source of our greatest strength.

JOYCE: Our wounds became the source of our greatest gifts, and it has been our joy to share our experience with others worldwide through retreats, our books, and our counseling services. We are living proof of the saying that we can all become stronger at the broken places.

25.

TOGETHER, ORDINARY PEOPLE CAN CREATE EXTRAORDINARY LIVES

Ken and Joyce Beck

Ken and Joyce have always viewed themselves as a simple, ordinary middle-class American couple. Both were products of traditional Midwest families, and they were high school sweethearts. Their original shared vision was not overly ambitious: to have a happy family life, a loving marriage, financial security, and fulfilling careers. But about twenty years into their marriage, they encountered a situation that they were ill prepared for. As a result of explosive growth in the high-tech company where Ken was employed, practically overnight they found themselves wealthier than they had ever imagined possible. Although some problems are more desirable than others, all major life changes require adjustment and adaptation. Neither Ken nor Joyce knew how they were going to use their newfound wealth, but one thing they were clear about was that they would not be the sole beneficiaries of their good fortune.

While the experience of receiving unexpected wealth is not unique to Ken and Joyce, what is unusual about their situation is that it not only changed the way that they lived but also, in a fundamental way, changed who they were. In realizing their vision of creating a world-class healing and growth center, they have fulfilled their personal goals and supported the healing, growth, and well-being of thousands of people across the country and throughout the world. What they experienced and created together would have been inconceivable to these two as teenagers.

KEN: Joyce and I were childhood sweethearts; we met when she was in seventh grade and I was in eighth. We started dating a year later. We stayed together through high school, but we went to different colleges. Being powerfully attracted to someone doesn't necessarily mean that person is "it." Sometimes it's just hormones. We both wanted to be sure there was more to it than that, and by our second year in college we knew there was.

JOYCE: When we first got married, Ken was extremely outgoing, and I was the opposite — very introverted. He was working his way up the corporate ladder at IBM and going to a lot of social events, which he loves, but I was uncomfortable in those situations. It was part of the culture we were living in, though, so it was a pretty steep learning curve for me. The vast differences in our personalities caused us a lot of difficulties during the early years of our marriage, before we learned how to deal with our differences more skillfully.

In the early seventies we took the Minnesota Couple Communication class, and it really helped us to improve the quality of our relationship. That was the beginning of the growth path that led us to where we are today. It helped us to appreciate that the ups and downs that couples inevitably go through are just part of the process and not necessarily problems that require correction.

KEN: For me, one of the most powerful teachings was to address issues when they come up, rather than put them on the back burner. I also learned how to speak from my experience instead of projecting judgments, making assumptions, or criticizing the other person. I learned that when I speak without blame, it's easier for Joyce to stay open to hearing me without being defensive.

Love is in the heart, not in the eye, of the beholder

JOYCE: Another major issue we've been through has to do with a health problem that I've dealt with for the past forty years. When I was eighteen, I was diagnosed with ulcerative colitis. I later had surgery and underwent an ileostomy, a procedure in which my entire large intestine was removed, which required me to wear a pouch outside of my body. This was a huge health problem for me and seriously affected my self-image. It was hard to see myself as physically desirable to Ken. He was unbelievably supportive during a time when I found it hard to accept myself. The love and care he gave me during that time enabled me to see myself as a lovable, worthwhile, and desirable person. I can't imagine what it would have been like if Ken hadn't given me the care and kindness that he did when I was in such physical and emotional pain. He helped me get over the shame and embarrassment that resulted from my situation.

KEN: Loving Joyce during her ordeal was the easy part. What was difficult and terrifying was the real possibility that I might lose her. She was very, very sick. Her condition was life threatening.

JOYCE: I was sick for nearly a year and spent several months in the hospital. When I got out, I was just skin and bones. During that time, Ken took over everything. He took care of our daughter, Gwen; he took care of me and the household, all while holding down a full-time job. I still don't know how he did it. I remember feeling terrified the first time we made love after the surgery. I felt disfigured and horribly unattractive. I hoped Ken wouldn't be repulsed by my condition, but I wasn't sure. He was so accepting at a time when I needed it most.

KEN: I felt so much love for Joyce that I couldn't help but respond to her with compassion and appreciation. It was easy to open my heart to her, and inconceivable for me to love her any less than I did before the surgery. If anything, my love and respect for her was even greater.

JOYCE: Another challenge we faced was the fact that the structure of corporate life doesn't really support families. The company relocated us many times during the first several years of our marriage, and that put an enormous amount of stress on the family. We lived in Milwaukee, Tulsa, San Jose, Rochester, Austin, and other places. With every move, Ken would go first; I would handle all the logistics of the move pretty much alone, since he was already gone.

KEN: It was much easier for me than for Joyce because I never left the security of the company. I stayed within the same culture; only the location changed. The new connections were already in place; I just had to step into them. And of course, Joyce was already established in her career as a therapist, so with each move, she had to sever her connections with the personal and professional community in which she was living and working, then start all over again somewhere else, perhaps on the other side of the country. She wasn't able to build her career the way I did; she had to keep starting all over again. One time it took her more than a year to get a job, and six weeks after she finally landed it, I got transferred out of state again.

JOYCE: Even when Ken wasn't getting transferred, there were problems because he was spending so much time traveling, mostly out of the country, and he wasn't around much to help me deal with things going on in our family. The company expected and required everyone, particularly high-level executives, to make the job their life, and of course that wreaks havoc in the family because there's nothing left to give anyone after the company has taken it all.

KEN: Balancing two careers and family was an enormous challenge for us, and it took a toll. If we hadn't learned what we did about communication and relationships early in our marriage, and practiced it, I seriously doubt we would have stayed together. I was in the corporate world for over twenty-five years. I was good at what I did, and the rewards were substantial, but the whole time I knew something important was missing. We both knew it had to do with giving back to our community — not just our neighborhood but also our larger community, a more global community. All my travel helped me see myself as a global citizen more than a local one.

JOYCE: Going through corporate marriage syndrome was a huge factor in our passion to create a growth center. We wanted to offer people who were living unbalanced lives an opportunity to change them. Establishing the center was a way for us to heal from the years of dysfunction we endured while Ken was giving his life to his work.

Although we received some great benefits from his work during that time, we also paid some huge prices for them, many of which we were unaware of until years later.

In the heady days of the tech boom, profits from Dell, where Ken was then working, went through the roof. With the company's profit-sharing plan and his stock holdings, he was bringing in more money than either of us had dreamed of having. All of a sudden we had a new problem: how to use all this money in the most responsible way.

KEN: Within a few years at my job, I was promoted to an executive position. We knew things were going to go big, but I had no idea how big.

JOYCE: As it became evident that we had more money than we knew what to do with, we realized how unprepared we were for the challenge of managing and sharing our wealth consciously and responsibly. We asked ourselves, "How can we make the best and most valuable contribution with our resources?"

Good problems are still problems

KEN: It may seem like a good problem to have, and it was, but it was still a problem. Joyce and I spent a lot of time discussing all our options, and we met regularly with friends to solicit their input. One day a friend suggested a retreat center. We liked the idea. The problem was that we each had a different idea of what the center should be. Over the years I'd been to a lot of corporate retreats, which were basically extended business meetings, and these usually took place in large, cold hotel rooms. I had always appreciated the value of the work we accomplished while on these getaways, but it seemed like more inviting settings would work better. My idea for the center was that it would be a place of natural beauty and warmth designed for business meetings and conferences. It immediately became apparent that Joyce had a different vision.

JOYCE: I wanted the focus to be on personal renewal and spirituality. Our friends helped us clarify our two visions for the center, and then we saw that it wasn't necessary to choose between them, that we could create a structure to hold both.

I had in mind a healing and wellness center where people could come for rest, healing, and personal growth, a literal retreat from the hectic world, where they could explore and nurture their inner lives and find peace, balance, and wholeness. In conceiving the center, Ken and I were influenced by our professional backgrounds, therapy and business. The center would incorporate both — two contexts for gathering, growing, and healing. We even came up with the perfect name for the facility. We would call it "The Crossings."

KEN: The challenge of cocreating what ultimately became a much bigger project than expected was huge! As soon as we realized what we wanted, and saw how we could make it happen, things got really exciting, and fun!

JOYCE: We put together a team made up mostly of friends, including an architect, a real estate agent, contractors, a land developer, a web designer, and a marketing person.

Whether different perspectives are complementary or divisive depends on whether you need to be right

KEN: Because of Joyce's career path and her deep hunger for her own personal growth, she was always going to workshops and seminars and bringing home more wisdom and knowledge than I would have found on my own. It's not that I don't value personal growth. I do, most of the time [laughs], but I'm just not predisposed to consider a growth-and-learning model. I see things more from a problem-solving orientation. But as Joyce grew in her ability to understand herself and communicate more effectively, I benefited from the information she brought home. At times, though, we were not able to get on the same page, when it seemed like the gap between us was too big and maybe the cost of our compromises was greater than the benefit we might experience from the process.

JOYCE: Our different orientations really became apparent while we were designing and building The Crossings. We brought to our planning meetings with the construction team the same commitment to effective communications that we had when dealing with family and personal issues.

KEN: I brought my own predisposition to managing and directing. I'd come dressed in my uniform — my business suit — and start issuing directives, usually without recognizing how the others were responding to them. After the meetings we would debrief each other, and Joyce would point out things going on that I was missing. Because I tend to be goal focused and task oriented, I miss a lot of the journey, and she helped me become more aware of people's subtler responses.

JOYCE: We utilized our respective strengths in the design process for the facility. Ken is left-brain oriented, and I'm more of a right-brain person. He's a linear thinker, strong in details, leadership, and structure. I'm geared toward sensing, feeling, and intuiting. We started each meeting with a check-in. This way we could see where people were and give everyone a chance to connect with the rest of the team. I also encouraged everyone to express their appreciation of the other members. At first the guys were uncomfortable with this "touchy-feely" stuff, but later on some of them told me they had never done anything like that before, and that they really appreciated that part of the meeting.

KEN: We had a budget I was committed to sticking to, but as in most building projects, the initial estimates of the amount of time and money required were lower, much lower, than what was actually needed. This created some serious financial challenges and required us to make changes in the design to avoid going too far over budget.

JOYCE: Another financial setback dealt a major blow to the project. Ken's stocks in his company, which were the primary source of funding for the project, began to precipitously drop in value. When we made the decision to build The Crossings, we had what we believed would be more than enough money to retire and create the center. But when the dot-com bubble burst in 1999, we were left with only a fourth of what we thought we would have. Still, we were already committed.

KEN: We had purchased the land and bought the materials and hired the subcontractors and construction crews, but the numbers no longer worked. I was committed, but that doesn't mean I wasn't scared. There were a lot of sleepless nights, nights when I would wake up and have no idea how we could possibly make this work. One night I woke Joyce up and I told her how afraid I was, and that we might have to quit, to hang up the whole project. She just looked at me and said, "Ken, we can't live our life in fear. We have to have faith that we're doing the right thing." There was such conviction, such quiet clarity in her voice, in her words, in her eyes, that I knew what she was saying was true.

I have a tendency to dwell on the negative, and Joyce reminds me of the positives when I'm caught in a downward spiral of negative thinking. That night was a turning point. From that time on, instead of wasting energy trying to answer the question "Should we stay with this or not?" I asked the questions "What do we need to do to handle this challenge? How can we make this work?" We did find a way of financing construction of The Crossings that really worked, one we hadn't seen when I was caught up in my fear.

I realize now that we're doing this not for ourselves but as an offering to a higher power, in service to something greater than our individual desires. And that's how each day is and continues to be.

The secret of life is: just don't quit

JOYCE: Sometimes it's just a matter of "keeping on keeping on." You just keep doing what you've been doing without continually second-guessing yourself. But it wasn't just the financial challenge that we were up against. We had different perspectives on the project, and these often created conflict between us. It was a hard time. But then I reminded myself of something I'd learned when I was a lot younger: that no matter who I was with, no matter what we were doing, there would be challenges, differences, problems in one form or another.

This reminder helped us create an agreement we still have, that whenever one person feels a need to discuss something, the other will always accommodate that need as soon as he or she can, no matter what. I've found that when we determine to come to a higher level of understanding with each other, practically without exception we're able to break through an impasse and come up with new possibilities we hadn't noticed before. But we have to be willing to really listen, to open up, to drop our defenses.

KEN: I knew from decades of working with Joyce that her judgment was good and that she was trustworthy. Her conviction that the center was meant to be, and the incredible support of the team members, helped me overcome what had felt like overwhelming doubts in a dark time.

We were upfront with the project manager and contractors about the financial crisis. We all pulled together to see how we could make it work. We came up with ways to build with good materials and an elegant aesthetic for far less money. Things began falling into place.

JOYCE: We had two different building contractors for the project, and one day we came to the work site to find a six-foot-tall chain-link fence down the middle of the property. I hung on the fence for a moment, looking through the mesh. It turns out that it's standard for a fence to be erected to prevent the crews from touching each other's tools and materials. I told them this operation was based on trust and respect for others and their property, and that I didn't care how things had been done before, that we were going to take down the fence. They thought I was nuts, but they agreed to do it. As it turned out, the two crews not only did not steal each other's tools but also ended up sharing materials and working together more cooperatively. They went from being competitors to operating as partners and cocreators. They shared their equipment, and their knowledge and skills as well. It gave us tremendous satisfaction to see them all working collaboratively. At the end of the project, one of the contractors said to me, "I am permanently changed by this experience. After this, I will never work the same way again."

Ken and I learned about sharing knowledge and power in this process too. At first we saw our different perspectives as problematic. But by the end of the project, we had come to appreciate the value of each other's perspective, and we were more interested in seeing each other's take on things than we were in trying to force our point of view on each other. I'm convinced that what we came up with while sharing the position of executive director was infinitely greater than what would have materialized had only one of us been in charge.

Because Ken's skills are so different from mine, it took me a while to see the value of his way of doing things and how good he is at what he does. We both now see our differences as complementary rather than as problems to be resolved.

KEN: I feel the exact same way about Joyce. I'm just in awe of how tuned in to people she is and what a difference it makes when they feel understood and respected and valued. I've learned so much from her about the human side of business and how it's related to the bottom line. It's not about becoming more like the other person; it's about becoming more authentically who you really are and honoring the differences with respect and appreciation.

JOYCE: What I keep coming back to is our sense of purpose, which is the foundation for all we do. At times when we wonder whether we can go forward, I think of all of the people who are with us, who have supported us and depended on us, and of our responsibility not to let those people down. Sometimes it feels like a heavy weight, but it's also a source of inspiration and strength that we draw on to stay true to our vision for ourselves, our family, and the world.

26.

LIFE'S ORDEALS CAN BECOME A SOURCE OF COMPASSION, INSPIRATION, AND LOVE

Riane Eisler and David Loye

Riane and David are two very passionate people, and their passion shows up not only in their marriage but also in the shared vision they have committed their lives to fulfilling. Despite differences in their personal, religious, educational, and career backgrounds, the foundation of their relationship is rock solid because it is grounded in a shared purpose. As a child, Riane was a refugee from Nazi Austria. She was among a small handful of people in her family not killed by the Nazis, and she spent the remainder of her childhood in the slums of Havana before emigrating to the United States. Riane has been an educator, attorney, human rights activist, public speaker, and bestselling author, and she currently serves as president of the Center for Partnership Studies.

David Loye grew up in an oil-baron enclave in Oklahoma and served in the navy during World War II. He earned a doctorate in psychology and taught at Princeton and the UCLA School of Medicine, and is the author of over twenty books.

Riane and David had each been married and divorced before meeting each other. Although they are aligned in their global vision, because of their differing styles and personalities they have different ideas about how to achieve these goals. Their differences have been the source of great stimulation and creativity as well as struggle. The fire that fuels their passion for social justice is also the fire that fuels their love for each other. Neither feels intimidated by powerful expressions of feelings. They challenge each other to more fully open their minds and hearts to new ways of seeing things, new ways of solving problems, and more creative responses to the concerns they share. They are each other's greatest support and provocateur: they continually prompt each other to go beyond their areas of comfort and familiarity to new, undiscovered territories of the mind and heart.

Because of her chaotic, displaced childhood, it is extremely important to Riane to have a stable and solid base from which to conduct her life's work, a place in which she can feel supported, loved, cared for, and, at times, challenged. Their marriage has proved to be the safe haven she needs. David describes their marriage as providing him with the sanctuary he needs to live in and return to while dealing with the challenge of living his life's intentions. Their relationship is both fiery and gentle, challenging and soothing, demanding and accepting. These two people have found that it's not despite their differences that they have achieved so much in their lives but because of them. Their differences have created a kind of complementarity that has given each a sense of wholeness. Perhaps as much as anything they have accomplished, this wholeness is their gift to the world.

Finding a life partner is both a science and an art

RIANE: I was forty-six and David was fifty-two when we met. We each had been married and divorced and had children from these earlier marriages. We've been together now for three decades, and these have been the best years of my life, as I found the partner I had dreamed of but had despaired of finding.

DAVID: At the time I met Riane, I was seriously looking for a life partner. As I'm a psychologist, I decided to design a scientific instrument to identify my perfect partner. It obviously couldn't be some long questionnaire I would haul out on a date, so I turned to my schooling in the Gene Webb technique of unobtrusive measures to reduce everything to just two questions. When I met Riane I could see immediately that she surpassed my criteria for beauty and intelligence. But would our relationship work? One bedrock criterion for my test was whether she loved her father. I knew that a woman who did would counter my pattern of withdrawing when we had a conflict. My first wife had hated her father; I had the same problem with my mother. This kind of problem drives couples apart rather than together when they're under pressure. I had to find someone more likely to pursue me, to insist we work things out. So the first question for my test was "Did you love your father?"

The second was based on boiling everything else bearing on potential compatibility down to a single question. My partner had to be someone with the same musical and artistic sensibilities. So I reduced everything to "Who is your favorite composer?" At that time for me, the answer had to be Mozart. I had to wait for the right moment and slip the questions in unobtrusively. I finally asked the "Did you love your father" question. When Riane said yes, this was a huge relief. But what would she say when I tried the second question? Slipping it into some seemingly innocent talk about classical music, I asked her, "Who's your favorite composer?" She said, "Why, Mozart, of course!" I knew I'd found the perfect mate.

RIANE: If I had known David was giving me tests, I don't think our relationship would have gone anywhere. But he did not confess this until much later. I, too, of course, had my standards. In getting to know David, I found him to be intelligent, poetic, physically attractive, and creative, and I loved his values. Another important thing about him was that he wasn't as egotistical as many men I had known. I was done with men who needed the world to revolve around them. I didn't know if I could find a man secure enough with himself to meet me as an equal — I had experienced despair and disappointment in so many of my other romances, and was determined to have equality in a relationship. I worried that perhaps I had painted myself into a corner with my new feminism and refusal to do what women have traditionally been expected to do — to massage men's egos and quite literally "stand behind their man." I wanted a real partner! And that's what I found in David.

Only you can determine whether your partner is a source of aggravation or inspiration

DAVID: I fell in love with Riane with wild abandon. The night we met, I drove back to her house and put my first love poem to her in her mailbox. Then I began writing a love poem a day to her. One day, when we'd been together for a few weeks, she said to me, "You know, these poems are so lovely they would make a wonderful book." I thought that was a great idea, but when she suggested the title "A Hundred Days of Love," I realized this meant I would have to write a poem every single day for a hundred days. I said I didn't see how I could possibly keep it up that long. She looked at me with a particular smile and said, "If you really love me, you can." There was something about that look and smile that worried me. I see now it was her test. Was she spoofing or was she serious?

RIANE: When I met David, I was quite ill. He showed me how much he really loved me, not only through his poems but also through his loving care. That was a major, indeed, *the* major factor in regaining my health.

DAVID: I come from a long line of caring men. My grandfather was a strong man, a top athlete, a man's man who smoked a big black cigar while he played poker. But he was an extraordinarily caring parent to his seven children. He bought all the groceries, hired the servants, and oversaw the preparation of meals to make sure the family was well nourished. His wife was emotionally shut down, so he was the go-to person whenever there was a hard decision to make or emotional difficulties. When I met Riane and realized she was very ill, I put everything else aside to monitor her health, going with her to all the doctors, quietly reducing all the stress points in her tangled life system at that time.

I felt, very simply, even back then, that she was someone with a special contribution to make to the world. I felt, somehow beyond reasoning, but as simply a fact, that it was my mission to see to it that she got well and got the support in her work she needed. We both had a lot to overcome. My parents created the appearance of being the perfect family. They were movie star beautiful. As children we were always brushed up and squeaky clean for the presentations and Christmas cards, but it was a sham, a shell. There was little real intimacy between my father and his children. He was outwardly affable but inwardly remote. And my mother was unpredictable. She could be warm and affectionate and, the next minute, turn on you in a rage. I never knew when the rug might be pulled out from under me. Over the years, with a lot of work, I believe our marriage has done wonders for us, healing the old childhood wounds of rejection and criticism that we both carried.

RIANE: Of course, we've both done a great deal of inner work. I perhaps more than David, as my wounds go so deep, way back to the shattering experience of having to flee the Nazis as a little girl, of my parents losing everything, of suddenly being plunged into poverty in an alien land. These traumas were very hard on both them and me. And although I am forever grateful for my two lovely daughters and now my wonderful grandchildren, all of which came from my first marriage, those fourteen years too were very difficult, not only for me but also for my children. My former husband and I were so incompatible that, when we divorced, it was as if a rubber band had stretched to its limits and broken.

DAVID: My first wife came out of a highly dysfunctional family. The two of us heartily agreed we'd bring up our children to know plenty of love. It was a conscious intention for us, no matter what. We had four children together. That marriage lasted twenty-five years; it worked for about the first fifteen years, then it went downhill. Although I believe we did succeed in giving our children plenty of love for a good bit of time, in the end it became hell on earth for both of us. I left that marriage yearning for the kind of loving connection with a partner I had never seen in my own family. Marriage seemed to be a matter of an initial love that eventually deteriorated into distance or conflict. Until I met Riane, I wasn't sure that anything else was possible. What I saw in her was what I'd been missing all my life.

I grew up in Oklahoma during the Depression. As a young man, I was a farmworker, bellhop, and oil field worker. During the Second World War, I served in the navy. When I got out, I became a newsman for radio stations and later for television. I moved to New York when I was thirty-five and became an account executive for a Madison Avenue advertising agency. But all that time, I was driven by a hunger to change the world for the better that obviously wasn't getting satisfied. So I went back to school at night, got my PhD in social psychology, taught at Princeton, and then, for nearly a decade, at the UCLA School of Medicine, I was the research director for the first major study on the effects of television on adults.

RIANE: My path was different from David's, but like him, from an early age I was driven by a passion to make the world a better place. This passion is rooted in my early experiences after the Nazis took over Austria, after the Austrian people voted almost unanimously to be annexed to Hitler's Germany, when their latent anti-Semitism broke out into terrorism against Jews. On the night of November 9, 1938, thousands of Nazis (both German and Austrian) rampaged through the streets of Vienna smashing and destroying the homes, businesses, and synagogues of the Jewish residents. It came to be known as Kristallnacht, Crystal Night, because so much glass was shattered by the Nazis as they rounded up, beat, and even killed Jews. On that night, a gang of Nazis dragged away my father. And it was only because of my mother's enormous courage, what I today call spiritual courage, or the courage to stand up against injustice out of love, that he was released. My mother was determined to fight for the return of her husband despite the fact that, because he was a Jew and an "enemy of the state," his release from captivity was all but impossible. She could easily have been killed. But she risked her life, and in the end my father was freed.

The weeks after his release were terrible. You could not get an exit permit unless you had a visa and passage out of Austria, and you could not get a visa without an exit permit. But because my parents had some means for bribery, we were able to flee, taking with us only what we could carry. We eventually left Europe for Cuba on one of the last ships of Jewish refugees permitted to land — before the *Saint Louis*, with almost a thousand Jewish women, men, and children, was forced to return to Europe because neither the Cuban authorities, nor any other nation in this hemisphere, including the United States, would let it land. We lived in the slums of Havana, and I later learned that nearly everyone in our family — grandparents, aunts, uncles, cousins — was murdered in the Holocaust, as would have happened to us had we not miraculously escaped.

Though they thought they could assimilate, as many Jews in Vienna thought, my parents had again experienced terrible persecution simply because they were Jews. I say *again*, because their trauma and displacement began before the Holocaust. My mother's family experienced an enormous amount of persecution and anti-Semitism during the early part of the century and during the First World War. I don't think that either of my parents ever recovered from the traumas they repeatedly endured. And the fear they carried made it hard for them to be unconditionally supportive of me. Of course, my sudden transformation from a protected child, secure in the love of my family, to a refugee in an alien land made a permanent mark on my psyche. But it also left me with a powerful commitment to building a better future.

I needed answers to a fundamental question: how could such terrible tragedies be prevented in the future? I needed to understand the underlying dynamics of violence and injustice. What kinds of social structures and cultural values did we need in order to support respectful, nonviolent, caring relationships? It was a long time before I came back to these questions, after I went to law school, after I worked as a social scientist, after my divorce, and after I became active in the women's liberation movement in the 1960s.

At that point I realized that just about everything I had been taught in my many sociology courses and texts left out no less than the female half of our species. When I then embarked on my own research, it was already clear to me that conventional social categories are of no use in answering the questions of my childhood. They all fail to take into account the whole of society.

Conventional sociology fails to recognize the importance of what children learn in families through gender and parent-child relations. I saw that, without also focusing on these relations, we can't understand social dynamics, much less build foundations for a better world. All of my work is basically about personal and cultural transformation, shifting from a domination model to a partnership model of social interactions.

In the early years, David and I often found ourselves in a painful situation. We had a classic "masculine" and "feminine" style of dealing with differences. My style was to put the issue on the table and deal with it, to work the issues out right away. David was not interested in dealing with things right away and had a tendency to be avoidant. He would say, "This is just the way I am." Sometimes he would even walk out of the room. My stance was "The hell with that, I'm here too!"

DAVID: One example of our differences is that I'm just not a very neat and orderly person. To be blunt, I'm sloppy, and, left to my own devices, we would probably be living in a pretty chaotic situation.

RIANE: I, on the other hand, require order and neatness in my living and working situation. Chaos drives me crazy. One of the reasons I need order has to do with the chaos and displacement I experienced as a child. This is an issue that we've really struggled with. Over time, we've both changed. David's become somewhat more considerate of my feelings and more willing to make a greater effort to clean up his messes, and I've become more willing to accept some degree of messiness. But we still struggle with this to this day.

I knew that many of our personal patterns grew out of a larger worldwide pattern stemming from the domination model, where men can make messes and women are supposed to clean them up. If you have the upper hand, you don't need to connect or even talk about

problems. There's no motivation to talk things out. Having internal-
ized the idea that "real masculinity" means being in control, many men
don't see the point in sharing power with another person. For me, it
was a matter of self-preservation to have a very different kind of relationship. I had to take a stand. This issue was more important than any
other in my marriage. My need to be seen and valued was paramount.

True partnership means sharing both responsibility and power

DAVID: After an argument, Riane and I are usually able to see that our
relationship is always the highest priority. Once we calm down, we tap
into the sense that it is going to work out somehow. I came to realize that
Riane was unwilling to sell herself out. She was in too much pain when
the issues were not dealt with. I realized that she was actually asking me
to make some changes and, at the same time, loving and cherishing me.
She persisted in expressing her discomfort, and I came to trust that she
was not doing this to attack me, but rather out of a commitment to her
own integrity as well as a commitment to our relationship.

It was hard for me to hear Riane when she raised her voice in anger
or outrage. I became anxious and shut down. But when she spoke in a
softer way, she was able to reach me. When I realized that my silence
and withdrawal were hurting her, I made up my mind to listen and try
to understand. I let go of the idea that I would stay to discuss an issue
only when I thought it reasonable. I began to understand that it was
important to show up and pay attention to her grievances whether I
thought they made sense or not.

RIANE: Eventually David got it that he needed to make a commitment
to engage the issues at hand and to understand how important it was to
me that we worked matters out. One of the most important things in
our relationship is our willingness to take responsibility for how we
might have contributed to misunderstandings. We're both generally
willing to look at our own part in things when difficulties arise and
apologize if we've inadvertently caused pain or harm to the other. It

kills me if I see that I've hurt David. It doesn't matter to me whether I'm right or wrong; as soon as I know he is hurt, I do whatever I can to heal our connection. I'm not a grudge holder. I never have been. David is a little slower to forgive than I am, but he's doing better.

DAVID: When we're at loggerheads, sometimes Riane can come around in just a minute or maybe two. It usually takes me a lot longer to let go of my anger. During that time, I usually withdraw. I don't do that to drive Riane crazy, which I know it sometimes does, but because I need that time to myself to quiet down.

RIANE: I've learned to trust that David will come back. He always does. I know he needs to experience the discomfort of his anger at me, and that pain is the motivating force that brings him back. It helps us both to remember that to a great extent the personal issues that arise between us are exacerbated by the flaws in our culture that promote divisiveness, fear, and mistrust between disparate groups — men and women, rich and poor, privileged and underprivileged — as well as between the dominant culture and groups characterized by ethnic and religious differences. While we're certainly dealing with our own personal issues, it's important to remember that we're dealing with them in a larger cultural context as well.

The willingness that David has demonstrated to really listen to me and take in what I say, to discuss things with me, to be influenced by me, is one of the most important things in my life. It started with my being willing to take a stand for what I just had to have in this relationship. I was for a long time in no way interested in marrying him or any man. My first marriage did not go well, and I was absolutely clear that I was unwilling to take on the baggage that goes with the identity of "wife." Even today, I don't like the word *wife* because of all the associated meanings of subservience to a husband that the term carries.

DAVID: And I don't like the word *husband* for the same reason.

RIANE: And so we lived together for almost ten years before we got married. In my mind, David wasn't perfect, but he had all the essential qualities I wanted in a man, and that was more than enough. He was and is attractive. There's chemistry between us. He's very intelligent. He's got great values. He's creative. And he loves and respects me.

In 1984 I was a part of a women's delegation for peace that went to the Soviet Union. Shortly before I left, a man came to visit us who had been living for many years with a woman he loved. He was desolate when she died, and said sadly, "People don't understand, because we were not married, the depth of our love and my loss." I began thinking about this and about other implications of choosing to stay unmarried. I decided we should get married before I left for the Soviet Union, and David agreed that it was time to do so.

DAVID: I've continued to write a love poem or two or three every year. But most important in our repertory is that, several times a day, I tell Riane how much I love and adore her, and she does the same for me. We all need reassurance, and the more we remind each other of our love, the more we trust and can relax into the depth of that love and keep recycling it back and forth. The longer Riane and I are together, the more gratitude we feel for what we have.

RIANE: In many ways it just keeps getting better over the years. I never thought it was possible, even though I desperately wanted it, to have a place where I could feel so completely safe and at home. My identity as an outsider was shaped by my childhood experiences of being a refugee. So finding my home — a place of belonging — has always been enormously important to me. Now I feel that I have finally found this home through David's love and unconditional acceptance. There's something else too: Our commitment to the common good is a huge bond between us. Our shared intention to try to bring about a better world is perhaps the most important element in our relationship, and it is part of the strong foundation of the partnership we continually affirm and create together.

DAVID: Out of our widely different backgrounds emerged the motivations for the lives that melded into what, together, became the theories and books we hope will make a difference. The aspect of our relationship I find most fascinating is how our love for each other widened into the kind of love that drives one to try to nurture, and when necessary, get out there and fight for, a better world. We may not succeed in creating the "perfect" relationship or in fundamentally changing the world, but I'll be happy if, at the end of our lives, we can say we fought the good fight as best we could, with zest and a sense of humor, and here and there did leave something better behind.

27.

AS LOVE GROWS, SO DOES THE SCOPE OF YOUR WORLD

Lynne and Bill Twist

To some people the notion of "making a difference" means writing to their congressperson or sending a donation to a worthy cause, or maybe attending a political demonstration. To Lynne and Bill Twist, it means quite a bit more than that. Although they come from very different backgrounds and have very different personalities, they have in common the passion to embrace with an extraordinarily fierce commitment any project they take on. They bring new meaning to the phrase "taking responsibility for making it happen." The two of them have a well-earned reputation in the nonprofit world as the people whose commitment to service is unquestionable, and whose word is as good as gold . . . literally. They have contributed over a million dollars of their own money to causes that support and empower people throughout the world. In addition, Lynne is a fund-raiser for projects dedicated to creating a thriving, just, and sustainable way of life for all, and has raised well over a hundred million dollars. She and her husband live their lives in a spirit of generosity.

When Lynne and Bill founded the Pachamama Alliance several years ago, it was with the intention to support and empower indigenous peoples in South America in preserving their culture and way of life and resisting the temptation to sell out to the transnational corporations that sought to exploit the rain forests and other natural resources of Ecuador, Bolivia, Brazil, and other South American countries.

The Twists have worked in a partnership that, for more than thirty years, has left a powerful imprint on the lives of vast numbers of individuals and families on several continents. In the process they've turned their home into a sanctuary that not only has served themselves and their three children but also has been a resting place for hundreds of people — from astronauts and international celebrities to indigenous native people who had never before left their jungle homes. There were bumps along the way, some of them small, and some big enough to tear apart even a strong marriage. Lynne and Bill's story illustrates what it looks like when two people integrate their personal work, their life's work, and their marriage into a foundation of commitment and integrity.

LYNNE: Bill and I met in 1961, when we were both students at Stanford. He was an upper classman and I was a freshman. Although we soon became friends and had a lot of friends in common, we didn't develop a romantic relationship until we had known each other for a couple of years.

BILL: Lynne had spent her junior year abroad studying in Florence, and we got together shortly after she came back from Italy. We went out for dinner together, and somehow it felt very different than it had between us in the past. Something happened that night. There was a major shift for both of us, and we began to see each other in a whole new way. From that night on, we went out every single night. We got married in December of my senior year; we just couldn't wait until we graduated. We lived in the married student housing for the last six months of school until graduation.

I grew up in Southern California and spent a lot of my childhood outdoors on sailboats. I have been sailing all my life. My grandfather came to California and started an English-style gentleman's club after making his money in England. He was a real sportsman. The Twists have always been involved with boats. We had a large extended family both in the United States and in England, and have always been a healthy, ambitious lot. We've always made our mark on the community wherever we've lived.

LYNNE: I've never encountered a healthier family than Bill's. There just isn't the drama that you find in most families. When Bill's youngest brother died in a car accident at age twenty-four, it was a great tragedy, and it was hard especially for Bill's mom, but the family just handled it. They didn't deny their feelings. They expressed them and supported each other. They don't allow any buildup of resentment or hurt that can explode later. I feel so fortunate to have married into this family.

BILL: I have such happy memories of going on vacation as a child with our whole extended family. I remember growing up feeling bathed in love, playing family games. It wasn't just the kids who played; the adults were playful too.

LYNNE: My grandfather was an engineer who made a fortune in Korea. My grandparents and my mother lived for years in Korea, which at that time was called the Hermit Kingdom. My grandmother lived like a colonial lady, and my mother as a child was treated like a little princess. But she didn't enjoy her lifestyle. What my mother really wanted as a child was to run and play with the Korean children her age, but she wasn't allowed to. The experience had a real impact on her, and as a mother she made sure that her own children would never be elevated and inflated. My mother had a strong drive to make up for her privileged, wealthy past, which she considered to have been exploitive.

Upon returning to the United States, my grandparents moved into a mansion on Broadway in San Francisco. My grandfather died when my mother was eighteen. My grandmother knew nothing about managing money, so she asked her brother, my great-uncle Frank, to handle the family fortune. He put everything into the stock market in 1928. The next year the stock market crashed, and the entire fortune was lost. My grandmother never spoke to her brother again.

My mother, who had developed a reputation for being a rebel, fell in love with my father, Griff Williams, who was a big-band leader. My parents were deliriously in love with each other, but when they got married it was a crushing blow to my grandmother, who did not want her daughter to marry a musician. I was the youngest of three girls, and I grew up in a home filled with music and dancing. My sisters were two and four years older than me, and we were all very close and happy nearly all the time. My mother joined my father on his road trips, but I never felt excluded from my parents' love and devotion to each other.

My childhood was like a sweet dream until the day I awoke to the news that my father had had a fatal heart attack during the night. There had been no warning, no struggle. All of a sudden, he was gone. He was only fifty-one years old, and my mother was just forty-seven. She went into a state of shock, and the whole family went into a tailspin.

I, too, was devastated by the loss of my father. I felt as if the ground under my feet had slipped away. In my efforts to find some solace from my grief, I immersed myself in religion. At that time, what mattered to me was being cool and popular. Being religious was definitely not cool. So when I went to Mass every morning before school to ease the pain of losing my father, it was all top secret. I hadn't really experienced much suffering in my life before my father died, and I had no idea how to deal with it. The church helped me get through the pain. Most of my friends did not suspect what was going on with me. But I was experiencing more pain than anyone knew. My suffering forged a rich inner life and greatly deepened my relationship with God. For a while I even thought seriously of becoming a nun, but ultimately decided against it.

BILL: When I met Lynne, we each immediately and vividly recognized that the other added a vital richness that had been missing in our own lives. Lynne exposed me to the world of music, art, and drama. I hadn't even known what I was missing. She taught me to appreciate the elegance and beauty in life that I had never known before.

LYNNE: We each have become more whole as a result of blending our differing styles and perspectives. We responded to the differences with curiosity and openness, rather than control or defensiveness, and we saw that what the other brought was life enhancing. We didn't even need to talk about it explicitly. Bill brought from his family a feeling of being grounded and solid, and I've always loved and appreciated that about him. I knew practically from the beginning that I wanted to marry Bill, but our true marriage didn't begin until years later, when we did the est training together. During that experience we both came to realize that we weren't fully committed to the marriage. It was a watershed event for both of us.

There had been a time early on, when our three children were small, that I suffered from feeling unworthy of Bill's love. He was brilliant and accomplished, and I was afraid that our marriage might not last. The training helped me realize who I was: my strengths, abilities, and talents. I saw that I could take full responsibility for developing myself if I was completely committed to my own development. The training gave me a strong sense of myself, as well as a confidence that Bill and I would make it together for a lifetime.

Commitment means there's no back door

BILL: Once we recognized that we would be together forever, we got down to addressing the issues of our relationship that had been on hold. After we had completely closed the back door and agreed that separation and divorce were no longer options, we realized that we had to work everything out. Putting problems or differences on the back burner, or hoping they would go away, was no longer an option for us.

We learned how to tell the truth to ourselves and each other, something we thought we had been doing, but really hadn't been. One of the first truths we had to acknowledge was that we'd been lying to ourselves about a lot of things. We scrutinized our behavior in order to catch ourselves when we were being manipulative. So many times we thought we were being straight and we really weren't.

LYNNE: One of the most valuable things we learned had to do with taking 100 percent responsibility. We learned how to "get off it." That doesn't mean disregarding your feelings, but instead tuning into what you feel in your body and noticing the experience. We learned how to get off our positions, and began to interact much more openly and generously. This teaching was similar to what my mother had said to me when I was a young woman. She had told me to find my husband "right," by which she meant I should focus on and affirm what was good about him, and never criticize. She told me to always uplift my husband, and that when he made a mistake to forgive him right away. My mother was from the school of thought that believed men don't grow up as fast as women do, and that, if their wives nourish them consistently, they mature more quickly. This guidance has been invaluable to me.

BILL: We also learned that being right is the booby prize. Telling the truth is the real goal. We were almost always surrounded by a lot of high-level support, and this made an incredible difference. Our network of friends was our church, our community. One of our basic values has always been service. We began to even more fully appreciate that there was much more to life than the fulfillment of our personal desires.

LYNNE: When I first heard Werner Erhard, the founder of est, say he was committed to solving world hunger, I burst into tears and couldn't stop crying. I knew this was what I was born to do with my life. I was reborn when the Hunger Project began.

BILL: Lynne was the number two person on the project, running the fund-raising and volunteer programs all over the world. She trained the volunteers and staff and was responsible for raising funds in forty-seven countries. She took the big donors on trips around the globe. Sometimes they found themselves sleeping on the ground in tents in places like Ethiopia, Zimbabwe, Bangladesh, and India.

LYNNE: It was an incredibly exciting and challenging time for us, and in some ways our relationship and family life paid a high price for the time I was away. During one of my extended overseas trips, Bill got involved with another woman and they had an affair. Of course I was initially very upset about it, but I realized quickly that my extended absences and neglect of Bill and our marriage had been a significant contributor to the affair. I was no innocent victim. There was no way that I could hold him entirely responsible for the situation; we both had played our parts in it. I never made Bill wrong for what he had done. I saw that I had pushed things too far by being away so much. In my absence Bill had found someone he could confide in. I eventually met this woman, and when I did I understood why he cared so deeply for her. She was a spectacular person.

My mother again helped me during this stressful time. She reminded me that good-looking, powerful men are always going to have temptation put in their paths. Women will naturally be attracted to them. My mother helped me see my complicity in being absent from the family. I came to realize that Bill and I had together created the context that had given rise to the affair. We had some work to do, and we got to it. I started to be more present in the marriage and to keep my professional commitment in its proper place. We were able to make the necessary corrections to reestablish our marital connection so that Bill wouldn't have to ever go outside the marriage again.

Marriage comes in many models

LYNNE: Almost as soon as things became more stable with us, we faced another challenge. It had to do with our family. When I first committed myself to the Hunger Project, the children were three, five, and seven. I was experiencing an inner struggle between the part of me who was committed to my mission and the part who thought I should be home with the children more. When I was away, Bill and our fabulous housekeeper managed the house and children. They did an incredible job. One day when I was feeling completely overwhelmed with guilt and inner turmoil, I called a family meeting. Our children, Billy, Summer, and Zachary, were all there. I told them why I was so upset, and I asked them how they felt about my continuing my work with the project. Summer, who at the time was seven years old, said, "Mom, if you can help to end world hunger, we don't want you to drive us to the orthodontist. And we have the coolest life. Other families go to Disneyland; we go to Bali. And we have all these interesting people coming to stay in our house."

BILL: This was another watershed event in our life. The children and I all hugged Lynne and told her how proud we were of her. I didn't feel deprived. I was still enjoying being in the business world and racing sailboats. We made a pact that if either of us noticed that anything was off, we wanted the other person to point it out. We have generally been very open to each other's feedback, and we each use it to look within ourselves to identify the deeper motivations in our actions. The more we have practiced giving and receiving this kind of feedback, the more our trust and confidence in each other has grown.

LYNNE: Bill has been very successful in business, and over the years we've been able to donate a great deal of our money to the Hunger Project. We saw that we didn't need to keep making more money, and realized that what we really wanted was to make more of a difference in the world. At that point we decided to make our home a sanctuary of acceptance and love.

Our home has become not only a landing and resting place for people from all over the world but also a kind of halfway house for those in transition in their lives, as well as a meeting place for all kinds of organizations doing wonderful work. One of those groups was formed right here in this living room. It arose out of an invitation that Bill and I received to go to Ecuador to meet with some native people who wanted to set up a facility for ecotourism in the jungle. Our group of twelve people was invited to a feast of wild boar. Later we were all invited to the shaman's home to participate in a ceremony using sacred medicine. When it was offered, Bill and I were the only two who stepped forward and chose to ingest it. Each of us individually saw visions of animals and plants. It was as if a veil had been lifted and we could see what had always been there. We were deeply touched by the visions we had during the ceremonies. There were profound spiritual teachings. When Bill and I look back on that night, we know that we experienced something together that was our joint destiny.

BILL: We made a commitment to assist these people in learning to deal with the outside world by means of fax machines and computers. After our return home, we showed our slides to friends, many of whom themselves later went to the ecolodge. More people made commitments to support the new organization, which led to more trips and more commitments. The movement kept building and took on a life of its own. After the first year, doctors were going down to help and a non-profit organization was set up. Now the foundation in Ecuador has become the largest organization in the entire Amazon.

Service is joy

LYNNE: We are known as the founders of the Pachamama Alliance. *Pachamama* means "Earth and Sky, Universe and All Time." But we feel that Pachamama has founded us. It has become what our life is about. Bill is the leader of Pachamama, and I stand with him. The Hunger Project was mine, and Bill stood by me. Pachamama is another chapter in our partnership. It is our calling. It is an alliance between the two of us and an alliance between Pachamama and other organizations. It is also an alliance between indigenous people and the modern world. The purpose of these alliances is to promote a sustainable future for all life.

BILL: We knew that, if we wanted to save the rain forest and preserve the indigenous way of life, we would have to work in the United States. It is about responding to what the world wants to happen, with more of a spiritual base. We've adopted a guiding principle from the indigenous people, who trust that the world will give you the messages you need to proceed.

LYNNE: There is a prophecy in the story of the eagle people and the condor people. The eagle people primarily rely on their minds: they are accomplished and wealthy, but still at risk. The condor people live primarily from the heart: they will reach a zenith, and their survival will be at risk. It is a positive prophecy of hope and possibility. Eventually both the eagle and the condor will fly in the same sky and bring the world into balance. This prophecy guides us.

I see Bill and myself as the eagle and condor. Bill is a successful, intellectual, competent businessman who reads voraciously. I shine in the world of spirit, prayer, and meditation, and operate from intuition and the heart. Years ago I resisted Bill's logical mind, and Bill used to get irritated by my flightiness. We have come to view these differences with a great respect, and over the years we have learned how to balance these two energies. We realize that we each need both, that one is not lesser than the other. This has made our marriage and our work together wonderful; we've learned to respect each other's qualities. And just as Bill and I have learned to deeply respect each other's styles, our civilization is challenged to do the same.

As great as things are, they can always be better

LYNNE: Forty years ago we honeymooned in Acapulco, Mexico. Friends of Bill's gave us their home and boat to use. Mario and his wife, Gloria, a wealthy Mexican couple with eleven children, were twenty-five years older than we were. We took them out to dinner to thank them for giving us this gracious gift, and at dinner Gloria noticed I was holding Bill's hand and putting my hand on his thigh. She leaned over to me and said, "You think you love him now, just wait twenty-five years — after having children together and going through hardships together, the love you have now will be so much deeper."

Gloria was giving me a blessing and creating my future. She was making a positive prophecy, a vision that marriage could get better and better over time. She was a woman I deeply admired and an important model for me, one who created a different context for me. She was so graceful and obviously happy with her life. Ever since then, whenever I go to a bridal shower, I pass that blessing along. I always tell the new bride that it can get better and better. On my twenty-fifth wedding anniversary, I called Gloria on the telephone to tell her that she was right. I also told her how much I appreciated her wisdom, and that she had been an important instrument in my arrival at the wonderful place I enjoyed in my life then. Her response to me was "Just wait until you're together for fifty years!"

APPENDIX

Featured Couples' Contact Information

Ken and Joyce Beck
The Crossings • www.thecrossingsaustin.com

Rich and Antra Borofsky
The Center for the Study of Relationships • www.beingtogether.com

Jim Brochu and Steve Schalchlin
www.bonusround.com • www.jimbrochu.com

Shakti and Rick Butler
www.world-trust.org

Barbara and Larry Dossey
www.dosseydossey.com

Ken and Maddy Dychtwald
Age Wave • www.agewave.com

Riane Eisler and David Loye
Center for Partnership Studies • www.partnershipway.org

Mariah and Ron Gladis
The Pennsylvania Gestalt Center for Psychotherapy and Training
www.gestaltcenter.com

Gay and Kathlyn Hendricks
The Hendricks Institute for Conscious Living • www.hendricks.com

Liza and Raz Ingrasci
Hoffman Institute • www.hoffmaninstitute.org

Hope and Laurence Juber
www.laurencejuber.com

Jane Morton and Michael Jacobs
www.ibreastfeeding.com • www.interactivewellness.com

Sara Nelson and Danny Sheehan
The New Paradigm Institute • www.romeroinstitute.org

Tom and Nancy O'Neill
www.squawvalleyinstitute.org

Jack Lee Rosenberg and Beverly Kitaen Morse
Rosenberg's Integrative Body Psychotherapy
Rosenberg-Kitaen Central Institute, Inc. • www.ibponline.com

Judith Sherven and Jim Sniechowski
www.absolutewrite.com

Maya and Barry Spector
www.barryandmayaspector.com

Hal and Sidra Stone
Voice Dialogue International
www.voicedialogue.org

Michael and Justine Toms

New Dimensions Radio • www.newdimensions.org

Lynne and Bill Twist

Pachamama Alliance • www.pachamama.org

Joyce and Barry Vissell

Shared Heart Foundation • www.sharedheart.org

ABOUT THE AUTHORS

Charlie Bloom, MSW, and Linda Bloom, LCSW, have been assisting individuals, couples, and organizations in the process of developing wholeness and integrity since 1975. They are the founders and codirectors of Bloomwork, and they have lectured and taught seminars on relationships since 1986 to thousands of people throughout the United States and in overseas locations, including China, Brazil, India, Japan, Indonesia, and Bangladesh. They are regular presenters at the Esalen Institute and the Kripalu Center for Yoga and Health. They have also served as adjunct faculty members and lecturers at the California Institute of Integral Studies, the Institute for Imaginal Studies, the University of California Berkeley Extension Program, Antioch University, the Omega Institute, John F. Kennedy University, and many other institutions of higher learning. Charlie and Linda have been married since 1972. They are the parents of grown children and are grandparents. They live in Northern California.

CONTACT US

We welcome your account of your own experiences in learning about love. Let us know if you are willing to include your story in one of our forthcoming books. We are also available for counseling and consulting services by phone. To receive our monthly newsletter or to get our workshop schedule or other information about our work, go to our website at www.bloomwork.com, contact us at

lcbloom@bloomwork.com,
or call 831-421-9822